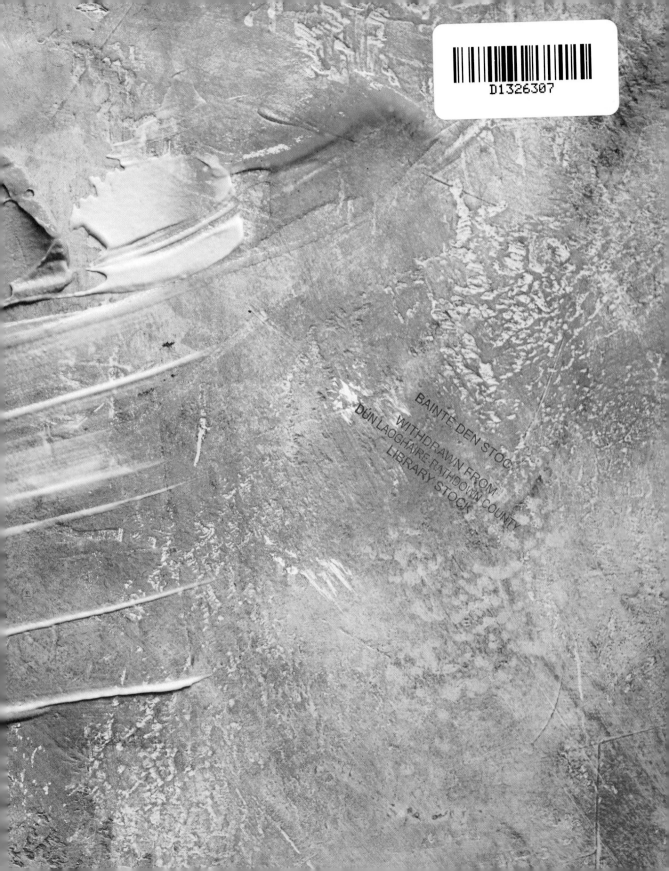

CREATE

BEAUTIFUL FOOD AT HOME

ADRIAN MARTIN

MERCIER PRESS

MERCIER PRESS

Cork

www.mercierpress.ie

© Adrian Martin, 2019

www.chefadrian.ie

Food styled by Adrian Martin

Photographed by Rob Kerkvliet
Prop styling by Zita Fox
www.afoxinthekitchen.com

ISBN: 978 1 78117 630 6

A CIP record for this title is available from the British Library

Printed and bound in the EU.

To my mum, Anne.

Thanks so much for being the best.

CONTENTS

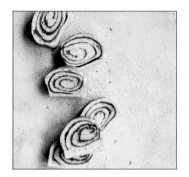

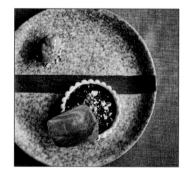

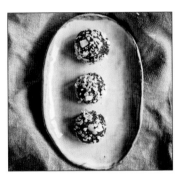

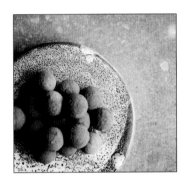

ACKNOWLEDGEMENTS

Firstly I'd like to thank you, the reader, for picking up my book and making a guy's dream come true. I hope you enjoy it.

I'd also like to thank my whole family, starting with my dad, John, for your great patience, advice, help and how much time you have invested in me. Thanks to my mum for putting up with all my messing; to my brothers and sister, Cathal, Sarah and Baby Seán; to all my cousins, aunts and uncles; and to my Granny Suzie and my other grandparents who are no longer with us.

I would not be where I am today without the support of a whole host of people. In no particular order I would like to thank them here:

Mary and Tom Whelan from KAL/Nordmende in Citywest, I appreciate all your support and help.

Everyone in Carton Brothers/Manor Farm – the best chicken comes from Cavan of course.

Martin Event Management, for being the best ever support and for working so hard at all my cookery demos and events across the country.

Eoin O'Flynn and everyone in Flogas.

Shane, Nicci and Matthew Smith from *Yes Chef* magazine, the Irish Hotel Awards, the *Yes Chef* Awards and Asian Food Awards. You guys rock!

All the Irish food producers who come to all our shows. A special mention must go to the Cavan ones: Clare and Ciaran from Moran's Mega Jam, Alan Raymond and his son Oisin from Ciste Milis, Barry John and Aaron from Barry John's Sausages, and John Rowe from Mr Muffin. Also, I'd like to give a special mention to Fionntán Gogarty from Wildwood Vinegars.

Martin, Muireann, Denise, Ray, Elizabeth and everyone in *The Six O'Clock Show* and everyone in TV3. Thank you for all the support through-out the years.

Marc Dillon, Robin Murray and Mark Boland from Nomos, who have put so much work into my TV shows. You guys are the kings when it comes to filming and editing.

My two best mates, Damien Timmins and Brian McAveety. I'm calling dibs on best man at both your weddings.

And finally, a special mention must go to my girlfriend, Fiona Coyne, and her family. Thank you for being there for me through everything.

INTRODUCTION

Food is something that keeps me up at night. I dream of the perfect, balanced recipe. I crave new ideas. I even wake up in the middle of the night to jot down notes. I go so far as to draw diagrams of different-shaped plates and where I will put each element of the food. I'll always create a dish, then serve and decorate it three different ways. To me, food presentation is art. It's like painting a picture. And I can always tell, out of the three different ways of decorating and presenting a plate of food that I design, which one really works.

Back when I started working in a kitchen, at the age of fourteen, I was obsessed with getting involved with the service side of things. So the faster I peeled and chopped those carrots, the more chance I had to observe what was being sent out to those 100 diners a night. I started in a restaurant at the higher end of the cuisine spectrum and was thrown right in at the deep end. Straight into fine dining. But it wasn't until the age of eighteen that I was given the chance to serve out the food myself, and when I was, I really found a way of expressing myself. This encouraged me to want to learn everything I could about food. I wanted to know it all.

This obsession has taught me so much and led me to some amazing experiences. Let me give you a few examples. I've been rabbit hunting with a pal of mine in Kildare, where I shot, skinned and cooked my own rabbit. I've been squid fishing in Donegal. As I'm sure you're aware, a squid's defence mechanism is to spray ink when threatened and, of course, I came back covered in the stuff! I've travelled to several butcher's shops, where I learned to butcher full animals and present them at the counter. It's amazing what you can do with a sharp knife. I also travelled to Clonakilty, to Bord Iascaigh Mhara, for two weeks, where I filleted thousands of fish and learned all the different techniques of a fishmonger. I could go on all day about things I've done and tried surrounding food, but if you think of something I might not have tried and probably should, then please don't hesitate to message me on Instagram or Facebook. Just search for Chef Adrian Martin and you'll find me.

When I got to the age of twenty-two, I reached a creative block. I was still working in someone else's restaurant, serving somebody else's food to which I wasn't able to add my own twist or spin. I found myself constantly questioning whether a certain ingredient would work better than the one I was having to use. Would a little bit of crème de cassis instead of brown sugar work better in that pickled beetroot? What if I served it a different way to how we were told to do it?

So, after six years in one restaurant, I moved to a one-Michelin-starred restaurant, where I was head of pastry. That excited me for all of 6–7 months. I then moved to another job, in a restaurant with two Michelin stars. Again, it excited me for a few months, but I soon found myself becoming bored once more with the repetition and frustrated at not being allowed to use my creativity. So I made the decision to jump out of the mould and take a chance. I chose to travel around Ireland, cooking what I wanted and showing schoolkids the basics, as well as teaching parents simple dishes. I then got the opportunity to cook on TV, where I now appear regularly. It was like someone said to me, 'Here are some ingredients, now go wild.' With the freedom of not working in a structured environment like a restaurant, I can create the dishes I want and experiment with flavours and combinations to come up with recipes that I love and I hope others will too.

In 2017 I got the chance to publish my first recipe book, *Fakeaway*, filled with my healthy take on the fast foods we all love. I'm delighted to now have the opportunity to write this, my second book. It's like a breath of fresh air for me. The point of the book is to teach you how to host the ultimate dinner party and show you how easy it can be to cook restaurant-standard food at home. I want to show you that it's not difficult to cook like this and that anyone can create amazing food. The secret is preparation, the mise en place which you can do the day before you host that dinner party or cook for your loved one. If you follow the instructions here, you will soon be preparing food fit for a king or queen, and I hope it will inspire you to try making your own perfect, balanced recipes.

Adrian

Author's Note: All the Celsius temperatures in this book are for a fan oven. If using a conventional oven you will need to increase the temperature by 20 degrees.

NECESSITIES FOR THE KITCHEN

Here are some items that will make your life much easier if you are making the recipes in this book. You will need to find yourself a really good kitchen store to source all of these, but it is worth the effort.

- Squeezy bottles (for purées, dressings, etc.)
- Tweezers (for picking herbs and micro salads, and for plating up)
- Fish tweezers (for removing fish bones)
- Small offset steel spatula
- Speed peeler
- Blowtorch
- Mandoline
- Fish slice
- Knives: chef, boning, tomato, serrated edge and flexi (for fish)
- Steel for sharpening knives and an oil stone for when they are very blunt
- Pasta strainer
- Kitchen tongs
- Different-sized melon ballers
- Ice-cream scoop
- A really good-quality food processor
- Oyster knife
- Ice-cream churner
- A stand mixer

HOW TO

How to Fillet a Fish

This skill takes time to get the hang of, but don't be afraid of it! You'll need a sharp flexi knife. Here, I am describing how to fillet a round fish (i.e. a salmon, sea trout or sea bass) – the easiest type to start with.

1. Before starting, dry the fish with some kitchen paper.
2. Scale the fish with the back of the knife if needed, by running the knife in swiping actions towards the head with a small bit of force so the scales fall off. Sometimes with salmon the scales are so small that you can leave them on and fire ahead.
3. Cut behind the gills, feeling for the collarbone with your knife and cutting along its length just behind it. You will be able to find the collarbone quite easily as it leaves a small indent behind the gills. Stop as soon as you feel the spine.
4. Run the knife along the spine all the way to the tail. Always follow along the bones.
5. To remove the fillet, pull the flesh back from where you made the incision along the spine as you run the knife closely over the ribs to the bottom of the fish.
6. Do the exact same on the other side.
7. Now trim your fillet up, removing any bits of fat from the belly and loose ends.
8. Pin bone with tweezers. You'll find if you run your hand along the flesh of the fish you will feel the bones. Most of the time they run up the middle to almost halfway from the side the head was on. Feel the bones and individually pluck them out with the tweezers.
9. Cut into nice-sized portions.

How to Shell Prawns

This is a simple but useful little skill. Be gentle and try not to break the prawns apart when you are doing this.

1. Twist the head off the body.
2. Crack the shell all along from top to tail gently.
3. Peel away the shell and legs in segments until you get to the tail.
4. Pinch the tail and gently pull the body out. Sometimes the vein will come out at this stage if you have the knack for it.
5. If the vein doesn't come out, score along the back with a knife to remove it.
6. Now the prawns are ready to prepare and cook however you like.

How to Shuck an Oyster

This one can be a little difficult at the start. You will need an oyster knife to do this. Be careful and watch your fingers and hands as you will need to use some force.

1. Wrap the oyster in a tea towel leaving the pointy end exposed. You'll find this end has a small lip into which you can wedge your oyster knife.
2. Wedge the knife into the lip with enough force to break into the oyster.
3. Twist the knife. This should open and loosen the top.
4. Carefully slide the knife along the top part of the shell to detach the oyster, and then discard that part of the shell.
5. Hold the bottom shell with the oyster in it flat, so that you retain the juice, as this adds the most insane flavour to sauces with fish. Carefully scrape the oyster itself into a container.
6. Once you have shucked all your oysters, they are ready for marinating, poaching, deep-frying or just eating right away.

How to Make Pasta

This recipe is one you will use over and over again. The key is to use good-quality free-range eggs. If you want a brighter yellow-coloured pasta use just the yolks. Each egg should be replaced with 2 yolks in this case. To make enough pasta for four people you should use 3 large free-range eggs and 300g Tipo '00' flour.

1. Place the flour on a board or in a bowl. Make a well in the centre and crack the eggs into it.
2. Beat the eggs with a fork until smooth.
3. Using the tips of your fingers, mix the eggs with the flour, incorporating a little at a time, until everything is combined.
4. Knead the pieces of dough together – with a bit of work and some love and attention they'll all bind together to give you one big, smooth lump of dough! There's no secret to kneading. You just have to bash the dough about a bit with your hands, squashing it into the table, reshaping it, pulling it, stretching it, squashing it again. You'll know when to stop – when your pasta starts to feel smooth and silky instead of rough and floury.
5. Wrap the dough in cling film and put it in the fridge to rest for at least half an hour before you use it. Make sure the cling film covers it well or it will dry out and go crusty round the edges. (This will give you crusty lumps

through your pasta when you roll it out, and nobody likes crusty lumps!)

6. Now it's ready for the pasta machine or rolling pin.

How to Make a Purée

A purée is used mainly in food plating for presentation, flavour and texture. It can really complement what you are serving it with. The basics are simple but please do not be afraid to explore different combinations of flavourings. Chefs normally keep their purées in squeezy bottles as they are much neater and easier to control that way (this is totally optional, however). Purées can be served hot or cold.

1. Pick a vegetable that really complements the protein you are serving the purée with. Sometimes it is good to choose one vegetable and serve it in different ways on one plate.

2. Peel and chop the vegetable.

3. Now you need to soften it, so start by boiling it in some sort of liquid. If it is cauliflower then boil it in milk, which keeps it super white. If it is any other vegetable, you would normally use salted water or stock.

4. Once your vegetable is softened so you can mash it easily with a fork, strain it.

5. Place it into a food processor with a good tablespoon of butter, a little seasoning and a dash of cream. Sometimes the cream may not be necessary so don't be afraid to hold back. This normally depends on the water content of the vegetable.

6. Blend until smooth and then pass through a sieve if you want it very smooth.

There are so many purées you can make, so please don't be afraid to try them out for yourself. Here are some examples of what purée is good with what meat:

· For confit duck leg: red cabbage purée (cooked in red wine and balsamic vinegar and then blended with butter and salt).

· For scallops: butternut squash purée (boiled in water, then blended with butter and salt).

· For braised beef: carrot purée (cooked in water with star anise, then blended with butter, cream and salt).

How to French Trim a Rack of Lamb

This cut is every chef's dream to prepare and cook. When done right it is the most visually appealing cut of meat ever. Sometimes this cut can be very fatty. Depending on what way you are serving it, you may want to trim the full layer of fat off the back. Normally, for herb-crusted lamb, you remove the full layer of fat and expose the eye (the circular piece of meat on the cut). If you are just frying off cutlets you would keep the layer of fat on so it naturally bastes the meat.

1. Using a sharp knife, cut through the fatty side of the rib right down to the bone from one end of the cut to the other. Now remove the layer of fat to expose the rib bones.
2. Use your knife to cut away any flesh that is sticking to the bones.
3. Scrape away any residual flesh on the exposed bones. Use a towel to wipe the bones clean. A great tip for really clean bones that is done in Michelin-starred restaurants is to use sandpaper to smooth them and then wipe with a damp cloth.

How to Break Down a Full Chicken

A great skill to know. You'll be surprised how quickly you can do this. If you want to cook a full chicken but don't have the time, this skill is very useful.

1. Start with the wings. Remove the tips between the joints. Once you have removed the wing tips, cut half the chicken wing off. I like to leave the inner wing bone on the breast but it's optional whether you remove it or not.
2. Now for the legs. This is a simple trick that allows you to take both legs off with one cut. Holding both legs by the top of the drumsticks, pull them towards yourself. Aiming sideways and away from your body, cut right through the middle backbone with your knife so that the two legs are held together by the backbone. After doing this, separate the legs into drumsticks and thighs.
3. Now for the breast. If you want it on the bone, cut right through the middle of the chicken backbone. If you want it off the bone, cut along and down the side of the backbone from one end to the other, as close as you can to the bone so you don't lose any meat.

BREADS

I believe it is always a nice touch, if you are having a dinner party, to have some freshly made bread ready as a complementary course before you serve your starter or amuse-bouche, much as you would find in many restaurants.

Brioche

A gorgeous, traditional, rich French bread that has a tender crumb. Traditionally served with pâté, foie gras and eggs Benedict, nowadays you'll also find it served as a burger bun. This recipe allows you to shape the bread whatever way you like, but here I am making a two-pound loaf that can be sliced and served to your guests.

MAKES 1 LOAF

INGREDIENTS

250g strong white flour, plus extra for dusting
3 pinches sea salt
2 tablespoons caster sugar
14g fresh yeast (use half the quantity if using dried yeast)
4 medium-sized free-range eggs
150g unsalted butter, cut into small cubes at room temperature
Olive oil for greasing

METHOD

Place the flour, salt, sugar and yeast in the bowl of your stand mixer, keeping the yeast away from the salt as it will damage its ability to ferment. Add the eggs and mix the ingredients with the dough hook attachment for 5 minutes on speed 1, until the eggs are completely incorporated.

Increase to speed 2 for a further 5 minutes until the dough comes away from the edge of the bowl.

Add the cubes of butter and continue to mix for 4–5 minutes until completely incorporated.

Place the dough onto a tray lined with grease-proof paper and flatten to 1–2cm in thickness with a spatula so it can chill evenly and quickly. Chill in the fridge for at least 30 minutes, until it isn't sticky.

Lightly oil a 2lb loaf tin, dust with flour and shake out the excess.

Once the dough has cooled so it is firm enough to handle, turn it out onto a floured work surface and shape into a cylinder that will fit into the loaf tin. Place it into the tin, lightly pat down with your hand so it is even on top, and leave at room temperature for 1 hour until it has doubled in size.

Preheat the oven to 200°C/425°F/gas mark 7. Bake for 20–25 minutes. It may take longer depending on your oven, so check with a skewer or small knife. If the skewer or knife comes out clean, then it's cooked. Remove the tin from the oven, slide the brioche onto a cooling rack and leave to cool. Do not cool it in the tin – it will steam and become wet if you do.

The brioche is now ready to serve.

Wheaten Bread

A traditional Irish staple. I've had so many different versions of wheaten bread but none tops this one. It has that little hit of sweet but also savoury at the same time. My tip for a nice crust and light centre is to half steam, half bake it.

MAKES 2 LOAVES

INGREDIENTS

500g coarse wholemeal flour
125g plain flour, plus extra for dusting
1 teaspoon bread soda
1 teaspoon salt
600ml buttermilk, plus a little extra if necessary
1 tablespoon brown sugar
1 tablespoon melted butter, plus extra for
    greasing
1 tablespoon golden syrup
1 tablespoon porridge oats

METHOD

Preheat the oven to 190°C/410°F/gas mark 6 and grease two 1lb loaf tins. Sift the flours, bread soda and salt into a bowl.

Make a well in the centre of the dry ingredients and add the buttermilk, brown sugar, melted butter and golden syrup. Using clean hands, mix gently and quickly until you have achieved a nice dropping consistency. Add a little bit more buttermilk if necessary – the mixture should bind together without being sloppy.

Divide the mixture equally between the loaf tins and sprinkle with the porridge oats. Most homes don't have an oven that can half steam and half bake, so bake these on the top shelf for 45–50 minutes with a tray of water in the bottom of the oven to create some steam. Check halfway through that the loaves aren't browning too much. If they are, reduce the temperature or move the loaves down a shelf.

To check that the loaves are properly cooked, tip each one out of the tin and tap the base. It should sound hollow. If it doesn't, return it to the oven for another 5 minutes. When cooked, tip out onto a wire rack and leave to cool completely.

White Bread Plait

(Braided Bread)

A gorgeous-looking bread that is sure to wow your guests. The recipe is very flexible in that you can shape it and change it by adding different flavourings to make alternative breads such as focaccia.

MAKES 1 LARGE LOAF OR 2 SMALL LOAVES

INGREDIENTS

500g strong white flour, plus extra for dusting

1 x 7g sachet of dried yeast

2 pinches of salt

2 pinches of caster sugar

325ml tepid water

Olive oil for greasing

1 egg, beaten

50g black and white sesame seeds

METHOD

Combine the flour, yeast, salt and sugar in a mixing bowl. Then pour in the water and mix with a fork until the dough comes together.

Tip the dough onto a work surface dusted with a bit of flour and knead for 10 minutes until well combined – when you press your finger into the dough it should spring back. The dough should be also be nice and smooth. Place it back into the mixing bowl and cover with cling film or a damp tea towel and allow to prove for an hour in a warm place.

After an hour, knock back the dough. To knock it back all you need to do is punch all the air out of the risen dough. Now you are ready to shape. You can make two small loaves or one large one. I like them smaller but it's entirely up to you.

For two loaves, cut the dough into six equal pieces. To be accurate, it helps to weigh the dough and then divide it by six. Roll each piece into a long strand. Each strand should be the same length. It helps if you have very little flour

on the surface so it forms a smooth strand. If you have too much flour on the surface remove some of it. Dampening your hands will also help you roll the dough out perfectly.

Preheat the oven to 190°C/410°F/gas mark 6.

Now it's time to plait. Take three strands. Place them parallel to each other and join the ends furthest from you together. Press them together so they hold and become one. Take the left-hand strand and fold it over the middle strand. Then take the right-hand strand and fold it over the first strand, which should be in the middle at this stage. Keep folding each side piece alternately over the middle piece until you reach the end. Ensure you keep the plait as tight as you can. Once the plait is complete press the ends of the strands together.

Place the bread onto a baking tray that has been greased with olive oil. Repeat with the second half of the dough.

Brush the plaits with the beaten egg. Sprinkle with the sesame seeds and bake for 15–20 minutes depending on the size. To check that the loaves are properly cooked, turn each one over and tap the base. It should sound hollow. If not, return to the oven for another 5 minutes.

I love serving this bread warm. I make it the day before, cool it down, wrap it in tinfoil and then reheat it in the oven at the same temperature it was cooked at for 10 minutes before serving.

Bacon and Onion Bread

I love a good-flavoured bread, where the flavouring is baked in. The bacon and onion combination is absolutely gorgeous in this one.

MAKES 1 LARGE LOAF OR 2 SMALL LOAVES

INGREDIENTS

500g strong white flour, plus extra for dusting

1 x 7g sachet of dried yeast

2 pinches of salt

2 pinches of caster sugar

325ml tepid water

Bacon and onion purée (see page 178)

Olive oil for greasing

1 egg yolk, beaten

METHOD

Combine all the dry ingredients in a mixing bowl. Then pour in the water and mix with a fork until the dough comes together.

Tip the dough onto a work surface dusted with a bit of flour and knead for 10 minutes until well combined – when you press your finger into the dough it should spring back. The dough should also be nice and smooth. Place it back into the mixing bowl and cover with cling film or a damp tea towel and allow to prove for an hour in a warm place.

After an hour knock back the dough. To knock it back all you need to do is punch all the air out of the risen dough. Now you are ready to shape. You can make either two small loaves or one large one. I like them smaller but it's entirely up to you.

To make one loaf, roll all the dough out into a flat rectangle on your work surface with a rolling pin. The length of the dough should be the same as the length of the tin you are using – do not go larger than a 2lb loaf tin. Spread the bacon and onion purée evenly across the dough with a palette knife.

Now roll the dough like a Swiss roll, nice and tight, and then seal the edges with your fingertips so it doesn't open in the oven. Grease the baking tin with a little olive oil and then set the bread into it. Cover with a damp tea towel and allow to prove for 15–20 minutes.

Preheat the oven to 180°C/400°F/gas mark 6.

Brush the beaten egg yolk over the whole surface and then place into the oven to bake for 40–45 minutes. To check that the loaf is properly cooked, tip it out of the tin and tap the base. It should sound hollow. If it doesn't, return to the oven for another 5 minutes.

Once cooked, tip the bread out and allow to cool on a wire rack before serving.

Olive Tapenade Bread

This olive tapenade bread works really nicely with the bacon and onion bread. Serve slices of the two together before any dinner party or special occasion to truly impress your guests.

MAKES 1 LARGE LOAF OR 2 SMALL LOAVES

INGREDIENTS

500g strong white flour, plus extra for dusting
7g instant yeast
2 pinches of salt
2 pinches of caster sugar
325ml tepid water
Olive tapenade (see page 181)
Olive oil for greasing
1 egg yolk, beaten

METHOD

Combine all the dry ingredients in a mixing bowl. Then pour in the water and mix with a fork until the dough comes together.

Tip the dough onto a work surface dusted with a bit of flour and knead for 10 minutes until well combined – when you press your finger into the dough it should spring back. The dough should also be nice and smooth. Place it back into the mixing bowl and cover with cling film or a damp tea towel and allow to prove for an hour in a warm place.

After an hour knock back the dough. To knock it back all you need to do is punch all the air out of the risen dough. Now you are ready to shape. You can make either two small loaves or one large one. I like them smaller but it's entirely up to you.

To make one loaf, roll all the dough out into a flat rectangle on your work surface with a rolling pin. The length of the dough should be the same as the length of the tin you are using, the largest tin you can use being a 2lb loaf tin. Spread the olive tapenade evenly across the whole dough with a palette knife.

Now roll the dough like a Swiss roll, nice and tight, and then seal the edges with your fingertips so it doesn't open in the oven. Grease the baking tin with a little olive oil and then set the bread into it. Cover with a damp tea towel and allow to prove for 15–20 minutes.

Preheat the oven to 180°C/400°F/gas mark 6.

Brush the beaten egg yolk over the whole surface and then place into the oven to bake for 40–45 minutes. To check that the loaf is properly cooked, tip it out of the tin and tap the base. It should sound hollow. If it doesn't, return to the oven for another 5 minutes.

Once cooked, tip the bread out and allow to cool on a wire rack before serving.

Ciabatta

This straightforward ciabatta recipe is relatively easy and satisfying to make. To get that classic ciabatta shape and open texture, you need a very wet and sloppy dough, so you really have to make it in a stand mixer. This thin-crusted, light-textured bread is perfect served warm with the wild mushroom velouté (see page 57).

MAKES 4

INGREDIENTS
500g strong white flour, plus extra for dusting
10g salt
10g instant yeast
40ml olive oil, plus extra for greasing
400ml tepid water
Fine semolina for dusting (optional)

METHOD
Lightly grease a 2–3-litre square plastic container with a little olive oil. (It is important to use a square tub as it helps shape the dough).

Put the flour, salt and yeast into the bowl of a mixer fitted with a dough hook, keeping the yeast away from the salt as it will damage its ability to ferment. Add the olive oil and three-quarters of the water and begin mixing on a slow speed.

As the dough starts to come together, slowly add the remaining water. Then mix for a further 5–8 minutes on a medium speed until the dough is smooth and stretchy.

Tip the dough into the prepared tub, cover with cling film and leave until at least doubled, even trebled, in size. This will take at least 1–2 hours, maybe longer.

Preheat your oven to 220°C/475°F/gas mark 9 and line two baking trays with baking parchment or silicone paper.

Dust your work surface heavily with flour – add some semolina too, if you have some. Carefully tip out the dough (it will be very wet) onto the work surface, trying to retain a rough square shape. Handle it gently so you keep as much air in the dough as possible. Coat the top of the dough with more flour and/or semolina. Cut the dough in half lengthways and then divide each half again so you have four even-sized pieces. Stretch each piece of dough lengthways a little and place on the baking trays.

Leave the ciabatta dough to rest for 10 minutes, then bake for 25 minutes, or until the loaves are golden brown and sound hollow when tapped on the base. Cool on a wire rack.

French Baguettes

This light, airy baguette has a wonderful crisp, golden crust. To get the right result, you need a relatively wet dough, which is why I recommend using a mixer.

MAKES 4 OR 5

INGREDIENTS

500g strong white flour, plus extra for dusting
10g salt
7g instant yeast
350ml tepid water
Olive oil for kneading and oiling

METHOD

Lightly oil a 2–3-litre square plastic container. (It is important to use a square tub as it helps shape the dough.)

Put the flour, salt and yeast into the bowl of a mixer fitted with a dough hook, keeping the yeast away from the salt as it will damage its ability to ferment. Add three-quarters of the water and begin mixing on a slow speed. As the dough starts to come together, slowly add the remaining water, then continue to mix on a medium speed for 5–7 minutes, until you have a glossy, elastic dough.

Tip the dough into the prepared tub. Cover with a tea towel and leave for about 1 hour until at least doubled in size.

Line two ordinary baking trays with baking parchment or silicone paper.

Coat the work surface with a little olive oil, then carefully tip the dough onto it. Handle it gently so you keep as much air in the dough as possible. This helps to create the irregular, airy texture of a really good baguette. The dough will be wet to the touch but still aerated.

Divide the dough into four or five pieces. Shape each piece into a sausage shape by flattening the dough out slightly and folding the sides in to the middle. The top should be smooth. Now, beginning in the middle, roll each sausage with your hands. Don't force it out by pressing heavily. Concentrate on the backwards and forwards movement and gently use the weight of your arms to roll out the dough to the length of your baking trays.

Place two or three baguettes on each tray. Cover each tray loosely with cling film and leave to prove for about 1 hour, until the dough has at least doubled in size and springs back quickly if you prod it lightly with your finger.

Towards the end of the proving period, preheat your oven to 220°C/475°F/gas mark 9 and put a roasting tray in the bottom to heat up.

When your baguettes are risen and light, dust them lightly with flour. Then slash each one three times on the diagonal along its length, using a razor blade or very sharp knife. Fill the roasting tray with hot water to create steam and put the bread into the oven. Bake for 25 minutes, or until the baguettes are golden brown and have a slight sheen. Cool on a wire rack before serving.

Soda Bread

Ireland's most famous bread is made with two of the oldest foods: wheat and buttermilk. The acid in the buttermilk reacts with the bicarbonate of soda and creates the rise. If you have kids you should teach them how to make soda bread, because it's great to be able to put a loaf on the table within 45 minutes. Once you've mastered this recipe, try adding some grated vintage Irish cheddar to it for a cheesy soda bread.

MAKES 1 SMALL LOAF

INGREDIENTS
250g plain white flour, plus extra for dusting
250g plain wholemeal flour
20g caster sugar
1 teaspoon salt
1 teaspoon bicarbonate of soda
400ml buttermilk

METHOD
Preheat the oven to 200°C/425°F/gas mark 7. Line a flat baking tray with baking parchment.

Put the flours, sugar, salt and bicarbonate of soda into a large bowl and mix well. Make a well in the centre and pour in half the buttermilk. Using your fingers or a round-bladed knife, draw the flour into the buttermilk. Continue to add the buttermilk until all the flour has been absorbed and you have a sticky dough. You may not need all the buttermilk – it depends on the flour you use.

Tip the dough out onto a lightly floured surface, shape it into a ball and flatten it slightly with the palm of your hand. It is important to work quickly, as once the buttermilk is added it begins to react with the bicarbonate of soda.

Put the dough onto the baking tray. Mark into quarters with a large, sharp knife, cutting deeply through the loaf, almost but not quite through to the base. Dust the top with flour.

Bake for 30 minutes, or until the loaf is golden brown and sounds hollow when tapped on the base. Leave to cool on a wire rack. Eat on the day of baking, or toast it the next day.

STARTERS

Scallops, Black Pudding

and Butternut Squash

An elegant starter that gets a beautiful balance from the meatiness of the black pudding, the sweetness of the scallops and butternut, and the crispy, salty texture of the Parma ham.

SERVES 2

INGREDIENTS

1 small butternut squash, peeled

200ml white wine vinegar

1 tablespoon caster sugar

½ teaspoon mixed peppercorns

½ teaspoon fennel seeds

1 tablespoon butter

100ml chicken stock or water

2 slices of Parma ham

6 large scallops, trimmed and row removed

Sea salt to season

2 tablespoons olive oil

6 thin slices of black pudding

TO GARNISH

Butternut squash purée (see page 175)

A handful of micro coriander

METHOD

First, prepare the squash. With a mandoline, slice the top half of the squash as thin as you can for the pickle. You will really only need five to six nice round slices. Place the slices in a jar or container.

Place the white wine vinegar, sugar, peppercorns and fennel seeds in a medium-sized saucepan and bring to the boil. Then pour this mixture over the squash slices, completely covering them. Allow to cool, then refrigerate.

With an extra-small melon baller, cut out ten little balls of butternut squash. Keep the rest of the squash for soups or even purée for this dish.

Place the butternut squash balls in a saucepan with the butter and stock, and cook on a really low heat for 3–4 minutes. Set aside and keep warm.

Place the Parma ham between two sheets of parchment paper and sandwich it between two trays. Place into a preheated oven at 190°C/410°F/gas mark 6 for 12–14 minutes until crisp. You can do this the day before.

Now you are ready for the scallops. Be prepared with a smoking-hot pan and have a tray lined with kitchen paper. You will need to work quickly with these. Once you have them cooked you will need to serve them right away, otherwise they will overcook and turn out like rubber.

Season the scallops with sea salt on both sides. Add the olive oil to the pan and, starting at the top of the pan, work your way around it, placing the side of the scallops you are going to present down on the pan, making sure the pan is absolutely smoking hot. Add in the black pudding. Each batch of scallops will be different sizes so there is no set time for cooking these. You will have to use your instincts. Check the first scallop you have placed to see if it is golden. If you are happy with the colour, quickly turn it. Repeat with the other scallops. Then turn the black pudding also, as it can cook very quickly.

Once you've turned the scallops and black pudding, be ready to remove them from the pan, normally after 30 seconds to 1 minute. Set on kitchen paper to drain and then serve immediately.

To plate, squeeze some butternut squash purée onto the plate, then add some slices of the pickle and finally the squash balls in a decorative way to the plate and garnish with the micro coriander. Place a scallop on the plate, then a piece of black pudding and repeat twice, arranging them in a line. Top with the crispy Parma ham.

Quail with Balsamic Lentils

Don't be put off by the quail in this recipe. It's a gorgeous poultry that's very sweet. In this recipe, you confit the legs – this allows the meat to fall off the bone and makes it melt in the mouth.

SERVES 4

INGREDIENTS

4 quail legs

200ml duck fat

1 tablespoon flour

1 egg, beaten

100g breadcrumbs

1 tablespoon sesame seeds

200g puy lentils

300ml good-quality balsamic vinegar

A handful of flat-leaf parsley, freshly chopped

4 quail eggs (optional)

4 medium-sized cèpe/porcini mushrooms
    (optional)

4 boneless quail breasts

Sea salt to season

2 tablespoons olive oil

50g butter

TO GARNISH

Spinach purée (see page 177)

Affilla cress

METHOD

Start with the quail legs as they will take the most time. An optional thing to do with them before any cooking is exposing the bone around the drumstick with a sharp knife. This is very similar to cleaning the bones of the French-trimmed rack of lamb (see page 26), but it's quite difficult to do with quail, so don't be afraid to leave it if you don't feel up to it.

Add the duck fat and the quail legs to a saucepan on a very low heat. Cover with tinfoil and allow to confit for an hour and a half, or until tender enough that the meat starts to pull away from the bone. You can test this by using a fork. Remember to keep this on a really low heat and don't allow the fat to boil.

Once they are cooked, remove the legs from the duck fat. Bring the fat to 180°C/355°F (check the heat using a thermometer), which is perfect for deep-frying.

In three separate bowls, place the flour, the egg, and the breadcrumbs mixed with the sesame seeds. Dip the quail legs in the flour, then the egg and then the breadcrumb mixture.

Deep fry in the duck fat for 3–4 minutes until

crispy, drain on some kitchen paper and keep warm until serving.

Place the lentils into a saucepan of salted boiling water and cook them on a medium simmering heat for 15–20 minutes until tender. Check them by having a taste – once they feel soft they are ready. Drain off all the water, then add the balsamic vinegar to the saucepan with the lentils. Cook the lentils in the vinegar on a really high heat until the vinegar reduces by half and becomes slightly thickened. The starch from the lentils will help thicken this. Add the chopped flat-leaf parsley and keep warm until serving.

Place the quail eggs, if using, into boiling water and set a timer for 2½ minutes. We want them soft in the centre. Once cooked, transfer them immediately into iced water to cool. Peel the shells off the eggs, rinsing with cold water if needed. Once peeled, cut them in half and refrigerate until needed.

Preheat the oven to 200°C/425°F/gas mark 7.

Cut the cèpes, if using, in half. Season both the quail breasts and cèpes with sea salt. Heat a large frying pan and, once smoking, add the olive oil. Place the quail breasts skin side down and the cèpes serving side down. Fry for 3–4 minutes on a high heat until golden and crisp (both the quail and the cèpes). Add the butter and turn down the heat to medium. Baste the quail and mushrooms with the butter, then turn them and fry for another minute. Transfer them to the oven and cook for 2–3 minutes. Try not to overcook the quail breasts – they can be served slightly pink in the centre.

Once the breasts and cèpes are cooked you are ready to serve. To plate, squeeze some spinach purée onto each plate, then spoon on some of the balsamic lentils. Arrange a quail leg and quail breast on top of each serving of lentils. If using, add 2 halves of a cèpe mushroom to each plate, then gently add a quail's egg. Finally garnish with some affilla cress before serving.

Prawns in Kataifi

with Lemon Mayonnaise

A delicious starter that is so simple to prepare and is quick to cook and serve. The pastry can be bought in the freezer section of any Asian market, but if you can't get it you can always slice some filo pastry with a knife. Micro salads can be found in specialised stores, or you can usually order them from your local fruit and veg shop.

SERVES 4

INGREDIENTS

100g Kataifi pastry (frozen)

Zest and juice of ½ lemon

3 tablespoons mayonnaise

2 tablespoons plain flour

Sea salt and freshly ground black pepper to season

1 egg

100ml milk

12 fresh Dublin Bay prawns

500ml sunflower oil

Mixed micro salad leaves

METHOD

Allow the pastry to thaw for 2 hours so that it's soft enough to work with.

Mix the lemon zest and juice and mayonnaise in a bowl and set aside until serving. Place the flour in a bowl and season with salt and pepper. Add the egg and milk to another bowl and whisk until combined.

Lay down twelve small individual bundles of Kataifi pastry on your work surface. Make sure to spread them out nicely. Dust the prawns in the seasoned flour, then dip them in the egg wash and wrap tightly in the pastry.

Put the sunflower oil into a deep saucepan over a high heat. Once the oil reaches 180°C/355°F (check this with a thermometer), deep-fry the prawns until crispy and cooked through, then drain on some kitchen paper.

Now you are ready to serve. Spoon a teaspoon of the lemon mayonnaise onto a plate. Arrange three prawns around the mayonnaise and then scatter the salad neatly between them.

Fried Oysters

The first time I had an oyster it was just down the hatch with no lemon or anything. It wasn't the greatest way of introducing me to them as I found it difficult to eat. This is a much nicer way of introducing you to this delicacy. Then you can become more adventurous and try them the traditional way.

SERVES 4

INGREDIENTS

500ml sunflower oil
6–8 oysters per person, shucked (retain the
    shells for serving)
Sea salt

FOR THE BATTER

Juice of 1 lemon
300ml beer
100g plain flour

FOR THE COATING

100g panko breadcrumbs
½ teaspoon garlic powder
½ teaspoon mild chilli powder
1 tablespoon sea salt

FOR THE DIP

4 tablespoons mayonnaise
½ teaspoon spicy harissa paste

METHOD

Mix the batter ingredients well with a whisk in a bowl until you have no lumps. Sometimes it helps to sieve the flour.

For the coating, combine and blend all the ingredients for 10–20 seconds in a food processor.

Heat the sunflower oil in a wok or large frying pan over a high heat until it reaches 180°C/355°F (check this with a thermometer). Dip each oyster in the batter, then the breadcrumb coating and place gently into the hot oil. Fry until crispy. This should take 1–2 minutes. Try not to overcrowd the pan. Drain on some kitchen paper and then season with a little salt.

Mix the dip together and you are ready to serve.

To plate, mix some sea salt with a tiny bit of water to soften it, and then place six small mounds of salt around a plate with some of the dip in a dish in the centre. Place an oyster shell on top of each salt mound, then lay a crispy oyster inside and enjoy them while hot.

Lobster Thermidor

This is such a classic recipe and is delicious as a small starter with mixed dressed salad leaves. Use the sauce sparingly as you don't want to overpower the lobsters' flavour. The sauce should just complement the shellfish.

SERVES 6

INGREDIENTS
Zest of 2 large oranges
1 teaspoon fennel seeds
3 x 2lb lobsters
200g Gruyère cheese, grated

FOR THE SAUCE
25g butter
1 shallot, finely chopped
275ml fish stock
55ml white wine
110ml double cream
½ teaspoon English mustard
2 tablespoons chopped parsley
Juice of ½ lemon
Sea salt to season

TO GARNISH
Basil purée (see page 178)
Red pepper purée (see page 177)

METHOD
Fill a large saucepan with water and bring it to the boil. Add in the orange zest and fennel seeds. Once the water is on a rolling boil, add in one lobster at a time and cook with a timer for 9 minutes, then refresh in some iced water.

Cut each lobster in half, splitting the tail down the middle, and remove the meat from the claws, tail and head. Set aside the meat and get rid of the empty claws and head. Chop the meat into nice pieces and place equal portions into the two halves of the tail shell.

Once all three of the lobsters are prepared, preheat the grill to a medium heat.

To make the sauce, place the butter into a pan over a medium heat. Add the chopped shallot and cook until softened. Pour in the stock, wine and double cream and bring to the boil. Reduce by half on a high heat, stirring occasionally. Add the mustard, parsley and lemon juice, then season with sea salt to taste.

Place the lobster tails on the grill pan and spoon the sauce over the meat. Sprinkle with the Gruyère cheese and grill for 3–4 minutes until it becomes nice and crispy. The lobster is now ready to serve.

To plate up, squeeze lines of the two purées on each plate and then add one half lobster tail per portion.

Wild Mushroom Velouté

Mushroom soup made from wild mushrooms has the most extraordinary, intense flavour. Don't be afraid to mix and match the mushrooms here. I find the more dark and old the mushroom, the nicer the soup. So don't be afraid of the dark ones while shopping.

SERVES 6

INGREDIENTS
25g dried porcini/cèpe mushrooms
150ml boiling water
25g butter
1 onion, finely chopped
2 garlic cloves, crushed
450g wild mushrooms (such as chanterelle, shiitake and oyster), sliced
1 litre chicken stock
150ml cream, extra to garnish
Sea salt to season
Fresh herbs to garnish

METHOD
To make the soup, soak the porcini mushrooms in the boiling water for 10 minutes. Drain, but be sure to reserve the liquid. Finely chop the rehydrated mushrooms and set aside.

Melt the butter in a large pan over a medium heat and gently cook the onion and garlic for 10 minutes, until softened but not coloured.

Increase the heat, add the wild mushrooms and stir-fry for 3–4 minutes, until just tender.

Pour in the stock and reserved porcini liquid, then add the rehydrated porcini mushrooms. Bring to the boil, then reduce the heat and simmer for 15–20 minutes, until the mushrooms are tender and the liquid has slightly reduced.

With a hand blender, pulse the soup until smooth. Add the cream and season to taste with sea salt. Bring the soup back to a simmer, then serve.

In restaurants we would froth the top of the soup like a cappuccino in a jug just before serving for visual effect and to make it lighter. Pour into a bowl, top with some cream and some fresh herbs, and serve.

Chicken and Mushroom Tortellini

A light, gorgeous starter that is so delicate and enjoyable on the palate. Every bite of these tortellini is more enjoyable than the first. I love making the pasta as it's so therapeutic, but if you don't want to go to the effort you can use wonton wrappers, which you can buy from the freezer section in most Asian markets. You can make these tortellini 1–2 days in advance for convenience: just blanch them in boiling water, refresh in ice-cold water and store on a tray in the fridge.

SERVES 6–8

INGREDIENTS

Fresh pasta dough (see page 24)

Red wine jus (see page 183)

½ onion, diced

2 cloves of garlic, chopped

2 tablespoons olive oil

100g wild/shiitake/chestnut mushrooms,
    diced nice and small

400g chicken mince

Sea salt and cracked black pepper to season

10g chopped flat-leaf parsley

2 tablespoons mascarpone cheese

2 eggs yolks, beaten

TO GARNISH

100g wild mushrooms (I use girolles)

1 teaspoon butter

2 tablespoons olive oil

1 head of bok choi, leaves cut off

Sea salt to season

Salad or herb of choice (I use chervil and
    edible flowers)

METHOD

Start by rolling out the pasta through a pasta machine or with a rolling pin into long thin pieces, until you can see your hand through the pasta. It needs to be this thin as it will expand when boiled.

Make the jus and pass it through a sieve. Set aside and keep warm.

Sauté the onion and garlic in the olive oil in a hot pan until soft. Now add in the diced mushrooms and cook on a high heat until softened. Add the mince to the pan and cook until you have achieved a nice golden colour. This normally takes about 10–12 minutes.

Put the mince mixture in a bowl and season nicely with sea salt and black pepper. Add the parsley and the mascarpone cheese. Mix well and taste the mixture to check the seasoning.

With a 7cm round cutter, cut out nice rounds of pasta. Place half a teaspoon of mixture into the centre and brush around one half of the edge of the pasta with egg yolk. Fold the tortellini into a half moon over itself, making sure you press out any air so the edges are sealed. Now all you have to do is place your little finger on the middle of the tortellini and wrap the two sides over it, pushing the edges together to seal. When you withdraw your finger there should be a small gap. Fold back the point on top of the tortellini to neaten it up.

Repeat until you have used the whole mixture. I normally serve three to six tortellini per portion. This mixture should give you enough to serve six to eight people.

To prepare the garnish, cut the mushrooms in half if they are big, although I like to use small girolles for this as they look and taste amazing. Sauté them in the butter and olive oil until cooked and softened. This normally takes 3–4 minutes on a high heat. Once the mushrooms are cooked, add the leaves of the bok choi on top and cook for around 30 seconds. Season nicely with sea salt and keep warm.

Now place the tortellini in a pot of boiling salted water and cook for 2–3 minutes or until al dente. If you are making these in advance, once cooked refresh them in iced water instantly and lay on a tray ready to reheat when serving. When ready to reheat, place them into boiling water for 1 minute.

To plate, start with the cooked bok choi leaves in the middle, lay the tortellini around them, drizzle over the jus, add the cooked wild mushrooms, then garnish with your salad of choice.

Crab Ravioli

This exquisite starter is one of my favourites from college. I love making every element, from the pasta to the flavoursome filling.

SERVES 8

INGREDIENTS

300g skinned salmon

2 pinches sea salt, plus extra to season

50ml cream

300g crab meat

Juice of ¼ lemon

A handful of basil and dill, chopped

Olive oil

Fresh pasta dough (see page 24)

Plain flour for dusting

1 egg yolk, beaten

TO GARNISH

8 large basil leaves

300ml sunflower/vegetable oil

Red pepper purée (see page 177)

8 oven-dried tomatoes (see page 183)

Extra virgin olive oil

METHOD

Put 100g of the salmon into a food processor with the 2 pinches of sea salt and blend to a smooth purée. With the motor running, trickle in the cream until it is blended. Transfer this mixture to a bowl, cover with cling film and chill for 20 minutes.

Finely dice the rest of the salmon, mix it with the crab meat in a separate bowl and chill for 20 minutes.

Fold enough of the salmon purée into the crab and salmon mix to bind it and then add the lemon juice and herbs. Season with sea salt. To check the seasoning, fry off a small piece of the mixture in a frying pan in a little olive oil until cooked, and taste.

Chill the mixture for another 20 minutes until firm, then shape it into eight nice neat balls, roughly 80g per portion.

Roll out the pasta using a pasta machine on number 8/9 or, if using a rolling pin, thin enough to see your fingertip through the pasta sheet. Transfer to a lightly floured surface and cut out sixteen 12cm rounds with a pastry cutter.

Place a ball of filling in the centre of half the rounds and then brush lightly around the edges of the pastry with the beaten egg yolk.

Place another round of pasta on top of each one and press the edges together to seal, stretching the dough slightly to mould it, so that there are no air pockets. Use scissors to cut around the ravioli to neaten the edges.

Blanch the ravioli in boiling salted water for 3–4 minutes and refresh in iced water to cool instantly. Put on a tray, cover with cling film and chill until ready to serve. You can make these a day in advance.

When ready to serve, reheat the ravioli in boiling salted water for 2–3 minutes. In the meantime, deep-fry the basil leaves in the hot oil for 10–20 seconds and drain on some kitchen paper.

To plate, drizzle a nice spiral of red pepper purée on the plate with a large dot in the middle. Lay one ravioli per portion on top of the large dot of purée. Add one oven-dried tomato on top and then top with a fried basil leaf. Drizzle over a small bit of extra virgin olive oil and serve.

Smoked Pork Belly

with Beetroot

A delicious starter that celebrates my favourite cut of pork. Sometimes the pork belly can be quite fatty, so ensure that you remove some of the fat after slow cooking. The beetroot will cut through the rest of the fat with its acidity. I use three different varieties of beetroot in this recipe as the colours are wonderful.

SERVES 6

INGREDIENTS
800g boneless smoked pork belly, skin on
8 sprigs of fresh thyme
2 tablespoons olive oil

FOR THE BEETROOT
3 whole beetroots (I use chioggia, deep red
    and golden varieties)
600ml white wine vinegar
300g caster sugar
6 crushed black peppercorns

FOR THE CRACKLING
1 teaspoon garlic powder
1 teaspoon mild chilli powder
Sea salt to season
500ml sunflower/vegetable oil

TO SERVE
Carrot and star anise purée (see page 176)

METHOD
Preheat the oven to 150°C/325°F/gas mark 3.

Place the smoked pork belly in a braising dish, scatter with the whole thyme stalks, and fill the tray with water until it covers the pork. Now cover it tightly with tinfoil and place into the oven to cook slowly for 3–4 hours. I highly recommend that you cook the pork the day before.

Remove the pork carefully from the braising juices (reserve to use as a stock for soup by cooling and storing in a container in the fridge). Remove the skin and keep for the crackling. If the cut is very fatty, remove some of the fat from the top.

Place the cooked pork on a baking sheet lined with cling film, then place another baking sheet on top with something on top to weigh it down. This will give the pork a firm, even shape. Allow to cool and refrigerate overnight.

Peel the beetroots and then, using an apple corer, cut perfect cylinders out of each one. You will need two pieces of each type of beetroot per portion, so six cylinders from each beetroot should do. Keep whatever you have left over for juices and purées.

Line up the cylinders on the chopping board and cut into twelve evenly sized pieces from each beetroot. I normally cut mine a little under an inch in thickness.

Pour the white wine vinegar into a saucepan and add the sugar and peppercorns. Add the beetroot pieces to this pickling liquid (they should be completely covered by the liquid) and place onto a medium heat to cook for 35–40 minutes, or until the beetroots have softened. You can check whether they are cooked using a small knife. Set aside until serving – they don't need to be hot for this.

For the crackling, scrape any fat off the pork skin with a small knife. Cut the skin down the middle and then cut into small strips about an inch thick. Place them into a bowl and season with the garlic powder, chilli powder and two good pinches of sea salt. Lay them onto a baking tray lined with baking parchment and place into a preheated oven at 50°C/160°F/gas mark ¼ for an hour and a half, or until they are dried out.

Heat the sunflower/vegetable oil in a deep-fat fryer to 180°C/355°F (check this using a thermometer) and fry small batches of the dried pork skin until it puffs up and becomes light and crisp. Drain on some kitchen paper and set aside until serving. You can make these a day in advance.

To finish the pork belly, once it's chilled and set, cut it into the desired portions. I normally get six out of the 800g. Heat a frying pan and fry the pork belly in the olive oil until nice and crisp on both sides. If the slices are very thick, finish heating them through in an oven at 180°C/400°F/gas mark 6 for 5 minutes.

To plate, lay the crispy pork belly on one side of the plate. Arrange two pieces of each of the beetroots on the other side. Squeeze or pipe on a nice dollop of the carrot purée to the side. Finally place a piece of the crispy crackling on top of the belly and serve.

Chicken Leg Terrine

with Celeriac Remoulade

This is a stunning chicken terrine, wrapped in salty Parma ham and paired with tangy pickled girolles. You can make the terrine in a traditional terrine mould if preferred, but the wonderful round shape here adds a visually striking touch to this classic dish.

SERVES 6

INGREDIENTS
2 large or 4 small chicken legs
4 sprigs of fresh thyme
Sea salt to season
500ml duck fat, melted
4–5 slices of Parma ham

FOR THE PICKLED GIROLLES
200g girolles
200ml water
1 pinch of caster sugar
80g runny honey
150ml white wine vinegar
1 pinch of sea salt

FOR THE REMOULADE
2 tablespoons mayonnaise
½ teaspoon wholegrain mustard
Juice of ¼ lemon
Sea salt and freshly ground black pepper to
    season
¼ celeriac, peeled

TO SERVE
Celeriac purée (see page 175)
20 nasturtium leaves

METHOD
Preheat the oven to 150°C/325°F/gas mark 3.

Put the chicken legs and fresh thyme sprigs into a braising dish. Season the chicken nicely with sea salt and then pour over the duck fat. Cover the dish tightly with tinfoil and place into the oven to cook slowly for 3–4 hours.

Once cooked, remove the chicken from the duck fat, discarding the thyme sprigs. Don't throw away the fat as you can use it again. Store it in a jar in the fridge.

Allow the chicken to cool slightly and then pick all the meat off the bones, removing the skin and any bits of fat. Try to pick the meat into nice small pieces. Place the chicken in a bowl and have a taste of it – season with some more sea salt if needed. Don't make it too salty as you are wrapping it in Parma ham.

To make the terrine, lay a large double layer of cling film flat on a work surface. Lay the slices of Parma ham, with the long side of the ham facing you and the edges overlapping slightly, down the middle of the cling film, making sure to leave

a 15cm gap around the edges of the cling film. The amount of chicken you have will determine how much ham you need. Add a large line of the chicken lengthways along the centre of the ham slices. Using the cling film as an aid, roll up the ham into a tight sausage shape. Refrigerate to set overnight.

Prepare the girolles by scraping from just below the gills to the bottom of the stalk with a small knife to clean any dirt off them. Brush lightly with a damp pastry brush to remove any remaining dirt and grit, and drain on kitchen paper. Put the water, sugar, honey, vinegar and salt in a small saucepan and bring to the boil. Remove from the heat, place the girolles in the liquid (they should be fully covered) and cover the pan with cling film to keep the heat in. Place in the fridge to pickle until cooled.

For the remoulade, mix the mayonnaise, mustard and lemon juice together thoroughly in a large bowl, with a generous sprinkling of salt and some freshly ground black pepper, so it all becomes one sauce. Slice the celeriac into really thin julienne matchsticks and mix these through the sauce. Place into the fridge until serving.

To plate, lay down a nice spoon of celeriac purée. Remove the cling film from the terrine and slice into portions about 2 cm wide. Place two pieces of the terrine on top of the purée. Arrange some of the remoulade and pickled girolles in a semi-circle around the terrine. Finish with some nasturtium leaves and serve.

Seared Foie Gras,

Sesame Seeds, Green Beans and Toasted Brioche

Gorgeously rich foie gras on buttery brioche bread is quite a simple one to put together, but you'll need to order the foie gras in advance from a quality butcher. When serving this, if you don't have basil purée, you can use a simple red wine jus spooned around the plate instead.

SERVES 4

INGREDIENTS

15 green beans, topped and tailed
1 tablespoon butter
200ml chicken stock
4 slices of brioche (see page 31)
4 x 60g slices of foie gras
Sea salt to season
1 tablespoon black sesame seeds
1 tablespoon white sesame seeds

TO SERVE

Basil purée to garnish (see page 178)
Micro salad to garnish

METHOD

Preheat the oven to 180°C/400°F/gas mark 6.

This is quite a quick one to prepare. Start by cutting the beans into inch-long portions. Blanch them in a pot of boiling salted water for a minute and then refresh by placing them into iced water.

Now get all your ingredients lined up and ready to go. Once you have done that, heat a small saucepan on a high heat, then add the butter, stock and beans. Bring to the boil and then lower to a simmer for 3 minutes. Toast the brioche and have it ready to serve.

Heat a dry frying pan and season the foie gras with sea salt. Lay the foie gras onto the hot pan and fry on both sides until you achieve a nice colour. You won't need any oil as it will release its own.

Mix the sesame seeds together and once the foie gras has enough colour, dip the serving side of the foie gras into the mixed sesame seeds. The seeds should stick nicely due to the fattiness of the foie gras. Transfer the foie gras to the oven on a baking tray, seed side up, to soften further for 3–4 minutes.

To serve, put the brioche in the middle of the plate. Lay the foie gras on top of the brioche and then arrange the beans in a criss-cross pattern around the outside. Squeeze or pipe the basil purée around the outside of the plate in dots. Finish with the micro leaves.

Carrot and Coconut Soup

Sometimes the simple things are just amazing as a starter. To keep everyone happy a good-flavoured soup can really hit the spot. French baguettes (page 39) or the white bread plait (page 32) both go really well with this.

SERVES 6

INGREDIENTS

1 onion, peeled and roughly chopped

4 sprigs of thyme, chopped

2 cloves of garlic, peeled and roughly chopped

2 tablespoons olive oil

900g carrots, peeled and chopped

1.25 litres chicken stock

400g tin of coconut milk

Sea salt to season

TO SERVE

200ml softly whipped cream

10g affilla cress

Crusty home-made bread

METHOD

Put a large saucepan on a high heat and sweat the onions, thyme and garlic in the olive oil until nicely softened.

Add in the chopped carrots and reduce the heat to medium. Sweat the carrots for around 10–15 minutes to release the maximum flavour from them. Add the chicken stock and bring to the boil. Reduce the heat to medium and allow to simmer until the carrots soften.

Once soft enough, blend with a hand blender. Once blended, add the coconut milk and return to the heat for 3–4 minutes. Season to taste with sea salt.

When serving this soup I like to give it a froth for presentation purposes. To do this, pour the soup into a jug and use the hand blender on a low speed with up and down motions to make the soup frothy.

Pour into a bowl and then top with a dollop of whipped cream. Place a piece of affilla cress on top of the cream and then serve with some crusty home-made bread.

Crumbed Boilie Goats' Cheese

with Apple and Hazelnut

An exceptionally gorgeous, light starter that will impress any guest. The apples complement the goats' cheese nicely and cut through the bitterness.

SERVES 4

INGREDIENTS

25g fresh white breadcrumbs

1 tablespoon finely chopped fresh flat-leaf
    parsley

1 tablespoon sesame seeds

Sea salt to season

1 egg

50ml milk

25g plain flour

12 boilie goats' cheese balls

500ml sunflower/vegetable oil

TO GARNISH

2 crisp eating apples

Juice of 1 lemon

TO SERVE

Apple purée (see page 176)

50g skinned, toasted hazelnuts, roughly
    chopped

A handful of rocket leaves

Extra virgin olive oil

METHOD

To prepare the crispy goats' cheese, mix the breadcrumbs with the parsley and sesame seeds in a shallow dish and season to taste. In a separate dish, beat the egg and milk together. Season the flour and place in another shallow dish.

Lightly coat the goats' cheese in the seasoned flour, then dip each ball into the beaten egg, gently shaking off any excess. Place into the breadcrumb mixture and turn until they are completely coated. Set on a baking sheet lined with parchment paper and place in the fridge for at least 10 minutes to firm up, or, if you are preparing these a day in advance, cover with cling film and leave until your guests arrive.

Preheat the oven to 180°C/400°F/gas mark 6.

Heat the sunflower/vegetable oil in a deep-sided pan or deep-fat fryer to 180°C/355°F and cook the breaded goats' cheese for 1–2 minutes, until golden brown. Carefully remove from the oil and transfer to a plate lined with kitchen paper to drain off any excess oil, then place into the oven for 2–3 minutes.

To prepare the garnish slice the apples thinly with a sharp knife. Toss the slices in the lemon juice to stop them discolouring.

To plate, lay dots of apple purée down in random places on the plate, then arrange three pieces of the crumbed goats' cheese around the plate. Arrange the apple slices in between the goats' cheese, then sprinkle with the toasted hazelnuts and sprinkle on the rocket. Drizzle with a small amount of extra virgin olive oil and serve.

Risotto

with Asparagus and Basil Purée

The basil in this dish gives a gorgeous flavour to the risotto combined with the Parmesan cheese. A good tip to remember is the old chefs' saying – a risotto boiled is a risotto spoiled.

SERVES 4

INGREDIENTS
1 onion, diced
2 cloves of garlic, crushed
2 tablespoons olive oil
300g Arborio rice
300ml white wine
1 litre vegetable stock
Sea salt to season
A big handful of frozen peas (or fresh if you
    can get them)
200ml basil purée (see page 178)
100ml cream
2 teaspoons butter
20g Parmesan cheese, grated

FOR THE ASPARAGUS
16 asparagus tips, trimmed
1 teaspoon butter
200ml vegetable stock

TO GARNISH
Balsamic gel (see page 184)
10g affilla cress

METHOD
Sweat the onion and garlic in the olive oil in a large, wide saucepan over a medium heat until soft.

Turn down the heat to low and then add the rice. Pour in the white wine and keep the heat low and allow to reduce down by more than half. Heat the stock in another saucepan.

When the wine is reduced, add two small ladlefuls of stock to the rice. Stir every now and again to stop it from sticking. Add in a ladleful of stock every time the liquid reduces on the rice and continue to stir until the small white grain in the centre of the rice has disappeared and you run out of stock. Season with sea salt to taste.

Stir in the peas, basil purée, cream and butter and cook for 1–2 minutes until the peas are heated through, stirring constantly. Finally stir in the Parmesan cheese.

For the asparagus, place all the ingredients into a small saucepan and cook on a medium heat for 2–3 minutes until tender.

To plate, spoon the risotto into a round cutter to hold a nice shape. Squeeze a few dots of the balsamic gel around the plate, then arrange the asparagus on top of the risotto in a criss-cross pattern and finish with the affilla cress.

Spring Rolls

Always a winner in my home place. My dad would eat ten of these at once. It's a simple starter but getting the presentation right really elevates this recipe, especially when entertaining guests. If you can't get your hands on spring roll wrappers, you can always use filo pastry. Just be careful it doesn't dry out while you are preparing these, so keep it under a damp cloth.

SERVES 4

INGREDIENTS
4 chicken breasts
A pinch of sea salt
1 tablespoon curry powder
Olive oil
½ red pepper
1 spring onion
4 tablespoons sweet chilli sauce
8 spring roll wrappers
1 egg, beaten
500ml sunflower/vegetable oil

FOR THE SALSA
½ fresh pineapple
1 bunch of chives
1 lime

TO GARNISH
Balsamic gel (see page 184)
Mango gel (see page 184)
3 teaspoons micro coriander

METHOD
Preheat the oven to 180°C/400°F/gas mark 6.

Put the chicken onto a baking tray and sprinkle with a pinch of salt and the curry powder, then drizzle with olive oil. Roast in the oven for 20–25 minutes.

Dice the red pepper nice and small, and slice the spring onion at an angle.

When the chicken is cooked through, allow it to cool slightly, then cut it into nice small chunks. Add the chicken, spring onion and red pepper to a bowl and drizzle in the sweet chilli sauce. Give it a really good mix with a spoon.

To make the salsa, dice up the pineapple really small, finely slice the chives and then zest and juice the lime. Mix all of these together really well in a bowl and set aside until serving.

Using two wrappers per roll to double wrap, to make sure they don't break while cooking, fill the spring roll wrappers with two tablespoons of the chicken mixture each, then roll the wrapper over the filling, tucking in each side as you do.

Brush the open edge of each spring roll with beaten egg to seal it so the rolls don't open while frying.

Deep-fry the spring rolls in the sunflower/vegetable oil on a high heat for 2–3 minutes until golden and crispy. Once cooked, drain on some kitchen paper.

To plate, squeeze or pipe the gels onto each plate and then spoon on a nice pile of the salsa. Slice each spring roll at an angle with a serrated knife into three so it can stand up. Stack the three pieces of one amazing spring roll on each plate, then finish with the micro coriander.

PALATE CLEANSERS

Blood Orange
and Thyme Sorbet

A strange one, but the sweetness of the thyme really complements the blood orange.

SERVES 6

INGREDIENTS
10 blood oranges
125g white sugar
5 sprigs of thyme, leaves picked and finely
   chopped
Juice of ½ lemon

METHOD
Grate the zest of two of the blood oranges into a large bowl. Roll each orange on the work surface to release the juice, then squeeze until you have 350ml juice. (I used nine in total, but as blood oranges vary in size, it is wise to have some spare.)

In a small pan, heat 100ml of the juice gently with the sugar, stirring to dissolve. Allow to cool slightly, then add the remaining juice, zest, chopped thyme and lemon juice and heat through for 3 minutes.

There are two methods of freezing the sorbet. For the best result I recommend using an ice-cream maker to churn. Allow it to churn until you have the consistency of scoopable sorbet, then transfer to a container and place in the freezer until you are ready to serve.

Alternatively, if you don't have an ice-cream maker, pour the liquid into a container. Cover and freeze for 45 minutes, then scoop the mixture into a blender jug and give it a few pulses to break it up. Return to the container and replace in the freezer. Repeat twice, then leave to freeze solid.

About 30 minutes before serving, transfer the sorbet to the fridge so it can be scooped easily. Serve a scoop per person.

Mango and Passion Fruit Granita

An icy, refreshing palate cleanser that creates a burst of flavour in your mouth.

SERVES 4–6

INGREDIENTS
4 mangos
6 passion fruit

METHOD
Place the flesh of the mangos in a food processor and pulse until smooth. Place the blended mango mixture and the pulp and juice of the passion fruit in a large bowl and stir to combine. Taste the mixture – if you find it too bitter you can add a little bit of sweetener, such as a small drizzle of honey.

Pour the mixture into a 20cm x 30cm baking tin lined with non-stick baking paper. Freeze overnight, or until firm.

Remove from the freezer when you are ready to serve and stand at room temperature for 10 minutes. Scrape the mixture with a fork until it forms nice ice particles, then spoon 2–3 tablespoons of the granita into each small serving glass and serve immediately.

Raspberry Jelly

with Vanilla Yoghurt

SERVES 4

INGREDIENTS

3 gelatine leaves

300ml freshly squeezed orange juice

150ml raspberry coulis (shop-bought)

25g caster sugar

200g natural yoghurt

1 vanilla pod, cut in half and seeds scraped
out

20g icing sugar

4 mint sprigs to garnish

METHOD

To make the jelly, start by soaking the gelatine in cold water. Set aside to soften.

Pour the orange juice into a large saucepan and add the raspberry coulis and caster sugar. Bring to the boil.

Take the soaked gelatine out of the water and gently squeeze dry. Add it to the boiling liquid and stir until it is completely dissolved. Set aside to cool slightly.

Pour the cooled jelly mix into four 200ml serving glasses, leaving about an inch of space at the top for pouring on the yoghurt once the jelly is set. Set in the fridge for 2 hours, or overnight. This jelly can be made up to 2 days in advance.

For the topping, whisk together the yoghurt and vanilla seeds in a bowl, then sieve in the icing sugar to take the bitterness out of the yoghurt and stir. Put the yoghurt into the fridge until needed.

To serve, spoon the vanilla yoghurt on top of the set jelly and then garnish with a mint sprig.

MAIN COURSES

Confit Duck Leg,

Five Spice Sauce and Crispy Root Vegetables

To confit is a French term for slow cooking meat, usually leg, to preserve it, developed at a time when there were no fridges.

SERVES 4

INGREDIENTS

4 duck legs

Sea salt to season

2 star anise

400g duck fat

1 carrot

1 parsnip

1 beetroot

2 tablespoons plain flour

500ml sunflower/vegetable oil

FOR THE SAUCE

½ glass of red wine

2 sprigs of thyme

1 tablespoon five spice

2 tablespoons honey

4 tablespoons balsamic vinegar

300ml beef stock

1 tablespoon cornflour, mixed with
    3 tablespoons water (optional)

TO SERVE

Red cabbage purée (see page 179)

Spinach purée (see page 177)

METHOD

Trim the duck legs the best you can by removing any loose fat, then season them heavily with sea salt, rubbing the salt in with your hands and covering the legs. Place the legs on a baking tray, add the star anise and cover in cling film. Leave for 2 hours minimum to cure, but it is better if you can leave these overnight.

Once cured, wash off the salt and pat the duck legs dry with some kitchen paper. Place in a casserole tray with the duck fat and star anise. Cover in tinfoil and place into a preheated oven at 150°C/325°F/gas mark 3 for 2 hours.

Once cooked, remove the legs from the fat. The fat can be used again – store it in a jar in the fridge and keep it for next time. Place the duck legs under a grill on a low heat to crisp for 10–15 minutes, making sure to keep an eye on them in case they burn.

To make the sauce, put the red wine and thyme into a medium-sized saucepan on a high heat. Allow it to reduce by half (this should take 3–4 minutes) before adding the five spice, honey and balsamic vinegar. Continue to reduce for another 5 minutes, then add the beef stock and either thicken by reduction or with the cornflour so it coats the back of a tablespoon. You can make the sauce the day before and reheat in a saucepan on a medium heat just before serving.

Peel nice thin strips of the carrot and parsnip with a vegetable peeler. With the beetroot, peel and slice it as thin as you can on a mandoline. Dust the vegetables with the flour. Heat the sunflower/vegetable oil in a pot to 180°C/355°F (check this with a thermometer) and fry the veggies until crisp. It's best to do these in small batches. It normally takes each batch about 3 minutes. I usually keep the beetroot until last, as it discolours the oil and, therefore, the other vegetables.

Drain on some kitchen paper and season with a touch of salt. These can be made a day in advance and served cold.

To plate, squeeze some red cabbage purée onto the plate for the duck to sit on. Place the duck leg on top, then spoon over some sauce, scatter the veggie crisps around it, and add a few squeezes of spinach purée to the plate to finish.

Herb-Crusted Rack of Lamb

with Sweet Potato

This was the cut of meat I most wanted to learn how to cook when training. If you don't want to do this yourself, your butcher will French-trim the rack for you. The Dijon mustard brushed on really complements the flavour of the lamb and allows the crust to stick.

MAKES 4

INGREDIENTS

2 racks of lamb cut in half (3 bones per serving)
Salt and cracked black pepper to season
Olive oil
2 tablespoons Dijon mustard
8 pearl onions
2 little gem lettuce, sliced thinly
1 tablespoon butter

FOR THE CRUST

4 slices of stale bread made into crumbs.
Small bunch of parsley
4 sprigs of thyme

FOR THE SWEET POTATO FONDANT

1 large sweet potato, peeled
2 tablespoons butter
300ml water
2 sprigs of thyme

TO SERVE

Carrot and star anise purée (see page 176)
Red wine jus (see page 183)

METHOD

Place the lamb on a chopping board fat side up. Lightly score the fat layer with a sharp knife. Next, generously sprinkle the lamb with salt and pepper. Mop up the excess seasoning with the meat, ensuring it is thoroughly coated.

Heat some oil in a frying pan on a high heat. Seal the lamb by placing each side in the oil long enough to develop colour. It is simple: no colour equals no taste, so make sure you brown the lamb properly.

Transfer the lamb to a preheated oven at 190°C/410°F/gas mark 6 and bake for 7–8 minutes. While the lamb is cooking you can prepare the crust.

Place all of the ingredients for the crust into a blender and pulse several times until it looks nice and green. Pour the mixture into a deep dish and set aside.

Remove the lamb from the oven and brush generously with the mustard. Dip the lamb into the crust mixture coating it completely. Dip it several times to ensure an even coating, then

allow the meat to rest for 10 minutes covered in tinfoil.

While the meat is resting make the fondant. Cut the sweet potato with a sharp knife so you are left with 2cm-thick rounds. With a 5cm fondant cutter, cut out four perfect rounds of sweet potato. Keep whatever is left over for a purée.

Add the sweet potato, 1 tablespoon of butter, water and thyme to a small frying pan. Cook on a medium heat for 5 minutes on each side until softened but not overcooked. Once cooked, pour away the liquid and cook the rounds in a little olive oil and the other tablespoon of butter with the pearl onions, until coloured on the outside.

Sauté the sliced little gem in a little olive oil, 1 tablespoon of butter and salt to taste for 30 seconds in a separate small saucepan on a high heat.

When you are almost ready to serve, place the lamb back into the oven for 3–4 minutes. Slice through each chop once ready. This is best served pink.

To plate up, put a little carrot and star anise purée and some of the little gem lettuce on a plate, then sit a portion of lamb on top. Add one piece of sweet potato fondant, a couple of pearl onions and spoon on the warm red wine jus.

Braised Beef Feather Blade,

Mushroom Ravioli and Burnt Onion with a Red Wine Jus

The beauty of this recipe is that it can all be done the night before. Then all you have to do is assemble it before serving. The burnt onion sounds strange but it works amazingly with this dish. It brings a perfect balance – if you leave it out you will find the dish is missing something.

SERVES 6–8

INGREDIENTS
1kg beef feather blade
Sea salt and black pepper to season
200ml red wine
900ml beef stock
2 good sprigs of rosemary and thyme
2 small onions
4 tablespoons olive oil
Red wine jus (see page 183)

FOR THE RAVIOLI
1 shallot, diced
500g mixed mushrooms, roughly chopped
2 tablespoons olive oil
200ml Madeira wine (optional)
100ml fresh cream
200g chicken mince
Fresh pasta dough (see page 24)
Egg yolk, beaten

FOR THE POTATO FONDANT
2 Maris Pipers, peeled
300ml chicken stock
100g butter

TO SERVE
Carrot and star anise purée (see page 176)

METHOD
Preheat the oven to 150°C/325°F/gas mark 3.

Place the beef feather blade into a large casserole dish. Season it well with salt and pepper, then add in the red wine, stock and herbs. Cover completely with tinfoil, making sure to seal all around so no steam can escape. Allow to slow cook in the oven for 2 hours.

When the beef is cooked, remove from the oven and cool slightly. Shred it into pieces on a double layer of cling film, removing any fat, and form into a sausage shape in the cling film. Squeeze and roll it so it holds the perfect shape. I like the beef to be around the same width as a medium-sized fillet steak. But it's entirely up to you what size you want it. You can control the size by squeezing in both ends of the cling film to make it thicker.

Place the meat in the fridge for a minimum of 3 hours, but preferably overnight, to firm up.

To make the ravioli, first cook the shallot and mushrooms in the olive oil until softened and coloured beautifully. Flambé the vegetables with the wine (if using), then add the cream. To flambé you can either tip the pan over your gas flame, or light a match over the pan. This basically cooks off the alcohol.

Remove from the heat and then, in a bowl, mix the cooked mushroom mixture into the chicken mince and season with salt and pepper. Roll the mixture into balls around the same size as half a table-tennis ball. Chill in the fridge while you roll out your pasta.

Roll out the pasta with a pasta machine, or, if you don't have one, a rolling pin. For this recipe you will need a long thin strip that you can see your hand through. With a 7cm round cutter, cut out twelve to sixteen rounds of pasta, depending on how many people you are serving.

Place one ball of the mixture into the centre of one round of pasta, then brush around the outside of the pasta lightly with the egg yolk. Place a second round on top and seal around the edge of the ravioli, making sure there are no air pockets. Repeat until you have six to eight ravioli.

Cook the ravioli for 3–4 minutes in boiling water until both the pasta and filling are just cooked through. Refresh in iced water and place on a plate with damp kitchen paper until needed. To reheat, just pop them back into boiling water for 1 minute.

To make the potato fondant, use an apple corer to cut out cylinders of potato. Cut the cylinders into small, equal portions, about 2cm in height.

Add the stock and butter to a pan over a medium heat and cook the cylinders on a simmer until softened – keep an eye on them to ensure they don't become too mushy. Once cooked, remove from the liquid to fry with the beef later.

To make the burnt onion, preheat the oven to 180°C/400°F/gas mark 6. Cut the onions in half, leaving the skins on. Add 2 tablespoons of olive oil to a really hot frying pan and fry the onions until they are burnt on the side you've faced down over a very high heat. Now place them into the oven for 3 minutes, then set aside to cool. Once cooled, peel out the individual layers carefully, discarding the skin.

To prepare the beef, once it is nicely chilled slice it into portions. Season each portion and fry each side over a high heat, along with the potato cylinders, in an ovenproof frying pan in 2 tablespoons of olive oil until both the beef and potatoes are golden. Once cooked, set the potato aside and keep warm until you are ready to plate.

Spoon 2–3 tablespoons of the red wine jus over the beef in the frying pan and heat gently in the oven for 10 minutes, basting the meat with the jus to glaze.

To plate, place a really good dollop of carrot and star anise purée in the middle of the plate and smooth it off with the back of a spoon. Put a portion of the beef on top of the purée, then one ravioli on top of the beef. Place some of the burnt onion and the potato fondants around the plate, and finally spoon over some warm jus.

Fillet of Beef with Potato Rosti

It's very hard to mess this one up. The sauce here has a nice combination of shallot and bacon mixed with the red wine jus to give it both a smoky and sweet flavour.

SERVES 2

INGREDIENTS

1 Maris Piper potato, peeled

Olive oil

Sea salt to season

2 large fillet steaks

Cracked black pepper to season

4 small banana shallots, peeled and halved

4 streaky smoked bacon rashers, cut into lardons

500ml red wine jus (see page 183)

4 handfuls of spinach

1 tablespoon butter

FOR PLATING

Celeriac purée (see page 175)

Spinach purée (see page 177)

METHOD

Start with the potato rosti. You can make these 2 or 3 days beforehand, wrap them in cling film tightly and store at room temperature. Run the peeled potato through a spiralizer. With a clean tea towel, squeeze out any moisture.

Place four blini pans onto a medium heat and fill each with 3 tablespoons of olive oil. Once the oil is hot, add in a small amount of potato so it covers the base of the pan. Press the potato down with a fork. I find using two forks is great for this job as it makes it easy for you to turn the potato. Cook one side for 3 minutes and then the other for the same amount of time. Once cooked, drain the rostis on some kitchen paper and then season from a height with sea salt. Set aside until needed. I normally stack them on a tray lined with kitchen paper and cover with cling film.

Ensure that the beef is at room temperature before you start to cook it by taking it out of the fridge 30 minutes before cooking.

Preheat the oven to 190°C/410°F/gas mark 6.

Heat an ovenproof frying pan on a high heat to get it smoking hot. Season the beef generously with sea salt and cracked black pepper all over. Add a little oil to the pan and cook the steak until a nice colour is achieved all over. Remember no colour equals no flavour. Once you are happy with the nice golden crust of colour, transfer the steak to the oven.

These timings will depend on thickness, so this is a rough guide.

> Rare: 2 minutes
> Medium rare: 3–4 minutes
> Medium: 5–6 minutes
> Medium well: 8–9 minutes
> Well done: 11–12 minutes

Once you have the steak cooked to your liking, allow it to rest. I find it easiest to cook the steaks before the dinner party and reheat them in the oven at 190°C/410°F/gas mark 6 just before serving for 4–5 minutes.

Place the same pan you cooked the steak in back onto the hob on a medium heat. Once the pan is hot, crisp and caramelise the shallots and bacon for 3–4 minutes in the steak juices. Once the shallots are golden and softened and the bacon is cooked, add the red wine jus to the pan. Heat through and remove from the heat.

Prepare the spinach by sautéing it in some oil, butter and salt on a high heat for 30 seconds to a minute. Drain it on some kitchen paper.

To plate up, spoon some celeriac purée on one side. Using a spoon, make a swipe through it and fill the gap with a small amount of the sauce from the bacon and shallots. Add the spinach purée to the other side of the plate and place a fillet steak on top of it. Spoon the shallots and bacon over the beef. Finally, lay some spinach on top of the beef and top with a potato rosti.

Turbot with Baby Courgette

and Stuffed Courgette Flower

This recipe takes great patience and precision, but the results are incredible. If you lay on the sliced courgettes neatly enough they will resemble scales on top of the fish.

SERVES 4

INGREDIENTS

4 turbot fillets (about 150g each), skinned

Sea salt to season

4 baby courgettes

2 tablespoons butter

400ml fish stock (see page 179)

2 sprigs of thyme

2 tablespoons olive oil

FOR THE COURGETTE FLOWERS

200g fresh salmon, skinned

1 teaspoon fresh ginger, peeled

50ml fresh cream

5 large basil leaves

Sea salt and black pepper to season

4 courgette flowers

200g plain flour

500ml sunflower/vegetable oil

FOR THE SAUCE

2 tablespoons olive oil

1 shallot, diced

2 cloves of garlic, finely chopped

¼ stick of lemon grass, bashed and chopped

2 teaspoons tomato purée

300ml fish stock (see page 179)

100ml coconut milk

Zest and juice of 1 small lemon

1 tablespoon sweet chilli sauce

100ml fresh cream

1 tablespoon cornflour, mixed with 3 table-
    spoons water (optional)

TO SERVE

Spinach purée (optional; see page 177)

METHOD

Start with the stuffing for the courgette flowers. Add the skinned salmon to a food processor, grate in the ginger and pour in the cream. Pulse until you have a nice smooth mousse. Chop the basil finely and then fold it in with a spatula. Season the mixture nicely with sea salt and pepper. Fry off a little piece of this mixture in a frying pan and taste it to make sure that it is seasoned enough.

Open up the courgette flowers and place a good tablespoon of the stuffing into each flower, being careful not to rip them. Alternatively you can place the mixture into a disposable piping bag and pipe some of the mixture into the flowers. Set the flowers on a tray, wrap in cling film and set aside until ready to cook.

To make the sauce, start with a medium-sized saucepan on a medium heat. Add the olive oil and fry the shallot, garlic and lemon grass until softened. This only takes about 1–2 minutes, so stay with the pot. Add in the tomato purée and sweat for 30 seconds, then add the stock and coconut milk and bring to the boil.

Add the zest and juice of the lemon, then the sweet chilli sauce. Bring to the boil again and then finish with the cream, boiling it for 1 minute. If you need to thicken the sauce you can either reduce it for a minute or two on a high heat, or thicken it instantly with the cornflour and water. Pass the sauce through a sieve and keep warm until ready to serve.

Preheat the oven to 180°C/400°F/gas mark 6.

Put the fish into a casserole dish and season nicely with sea salt. Slice the baby courgettes thinly through a mandoline so you are left with nice rounds. In a pot of boiling salted water cook the courgette slices for 30 seconds and then refresh them in iced water to stop them cooking further. Lay the sliced courgettes on top of the fish portions neatly and precisely so they resemble fish scales.

Melt the butter in a saucepan on a medium heat and then pour in the fish stock to create an emulsion. Add the thyme to the liquid and then pour it all around the prepared turbot. Drizzle the courgettes you've layered on top of the fish with the olive oil and bake the fish in the oven for 8–10 minutes depending on thickness. Be careful not to overcook the fish. When cooked, spoon the liquid over the top to give it a nice shine.

While the fish is cooking fry the courgette flowers. Make a simple batter of 100ml water and 100g of the flour in a bowl, whisking to make sure you have no lumps. Place the other 100g of flour in a second bowl. Dust the stuffed courgette flowers in this flour, then dip into the batter. Deep-fry in the hot sunflower/vegetable oil until nice and crisp on the outside, making sure that the stuffing is cooked in the middle. They normally take 3–4 minutes to fry. You are looking for a nice golden colour and a light texture.

To plate, place a portion of turbot with its courgette scales on the plate, making sure to be very careful that the courgette doesn't come off. Next spoon on the sauce to one side of the flower. Finally place the flower next to the fish. I like to use spinach purée as a garnish on this dish, but it is totally optional.

Vegetable Spring Rolls

with Fried Parmesan Polenta

A gorgeous main course, I absolutely adore polenta fried like this. You can also use the leftovers of the polenta and fry it into chips days after your meal. If you can't get your hands on spring roll wrappers, you can always use filo pastry. Just be careful it doesn't dry out while you are preparing these, so keep it under a damp cloth.

SERVES 4

INGREDIENTS

FOR THE POLENTA

400ml vegetable stock

150g quick-cook polenta, plus 2 tablespoons
    for dusting

A pinch of sea salt

40g Parmesan cheese, plus extra to serve

2 teaspoons dried oregano

Butter for greasing

FOR THE SPRING ROLLS

6–8 Chantenay carrots, top, tailed and halved

100g baby leeks, cut in half

100g asparagus tips, cut into small pieces

2 tablespoons olive oil

Sea salt to season

1 avocado, peeled, destoned and roughly
    chopped

300ml red pepper purée (see page 177)

8 spring roll wrappers

1 egg, beaten

500ml sunflower/vegetable oil

TO GARNISH

Red pepper purée (see page 177)

Basil purée (see page 178)

Oven-dried tomatoes (see page 183)

10g affilla cress

METHOD

Start with the polenta. Bring the stock to the boil and slowly whisk in the polenta, stirring constantly. Add a pinch of sea salt and, after a few minutes, once thickened, finely grate in the Parmesan and stir in the oregano. Pour into a 20cm square tin greased with butter and lined with cling film, and pop in the fridge to chill and firm up for about 1 hour.

Cut the chilled polenta with a 5cm pastry cutter into nice rounds. Dust with the extra polenta. Keep chilled until you are frying the spring rolls.

For the spring rolls, start by boiling the Chantenay carrots in salted water for 6–8 minutes until nice and soft. Once cooked refresh them in some iced water.

Cook the leeks and asparagus in a frying pan in the olive oil on a medium heat until softened and slightly coloured. Add the carrots and cook for another minute. Season lightly with sea salt. Now remove from the heat and stir in the avocado and red pepper purée.

Using two wrappers per roll, fill four spring rolls with two heaped tablespoons of the vegetable mixture each, then roll the wrapper over the filling, tucking in each side as you do. This double wrap is to make sure they don't break while cooking. Brush the open edge of the spring roll with the beaten egg to seal, so the rolls don't open while frying.

Deep-fry the spring rolls and the polenta rounds in the sunflower/vegetable oil on a high heat for 2–3 minutes until golden and crispy. Once cooked, drain on some kitchen paper.

To plate, cut the spring rolls with a serrated-edge knife into three pieces at an angle so they will stand up on the plate. Decorate the plate with the red pepper and basil purées, then add the three slices of spring roll, followed by a portion of the crispy polenta. Grate the extra Parmesan over the polenta. Finally sit the oven-dried tomatoes on top of the polenta and finish with 2–3 pieces of affilla cress.

Wild Sea Trout,

Red Pepper Orzo and Glazed Beetroot with Baby Vegetables

I love sea trout. Its flavour is very subtle and sweet. We can eat lots of this fish as it is not under threat. Try to sub it in for salmon when you can. I love it with a crispy skin. Orzo looks quite like rice, but is a pasta, so be careful not to overcook it. It's a great carrier of flavour.

SERVES 2

INGREDIENTS

2 small beetroot

Olive oil

6 asparagus spears

1 baby courgette

40g sea samphire

2 tablespoons butter

400ml fish stock (see page 179)

Sea salt to season

100g orzo

40g red pepper purée (see page 177), plus
    extra for serving

200ml cherry (or ordinary) balsamic vinegar

2 x 150g fillets of sea trout, skin on

2 sprigs of thyme

TO SERVE (OPTIONAL)

Spinach purée (see page 177)

METHOD

Preheat the oven to 180°C/400°F/gas mark 6.

Start with the beetroot. Cut off the long green stalks, but not too close to the root or their colour will bleed, then rub them with some olive oil and wrap them in tinfoil. Place them onto a baking tray and roast in the oven until softened. Small beetroots take around 35 minutes. You'll know they are cooked as they will be soft – to test this you can pierce them with a small, sharp knife.

In the meantime prepare the baby vegetables. All we want are the tips of the asparagus, so cut off the stalks (these can be kept for soups and stocks). Slice the courgette into nice thin rounds with a knife. Pick the bottom stalks off the sea samphire as these can be very chewy. Once you have these prepared, place them all into a small saucepan and add in 1 tablespoon of butter and 200ml of fish stock. Season with a small pinch of sea salt and set aside.

Add the orzo to a pot of boiling salted water and cook it according to the packet instructions. Once cooked, drain off the water and stir the red

pepper purée through the orzo. Season to taste with sea salt and keep warm.

Remove the beetroots from the oven and peel off the skin with a small knife. I recommend wearing disposable gloves when doing this. Cut the beetroots into segments. Heat a small frying pan nice and hot, then add the balsamic vinegar and beetroot segments. Allow the beetroot segments to go sticky and glazed. This normally takes 2–3 minutes. Set aside and keep warm.

Score the skin of the fish and pat it dry with kitchen paper. This allows the fish to become extra crispy. Heat a pan until it is smoking hot. At this stage you can put your baby vegetables on to simmer for 3–4 minutes. Season the fish with sea salt on both sides. Add 2 tablespoons of olive oil to the pan and place the fish into it, skin side down. You'll need to press the flesh down so that the skin gets full contact with the pan, as otherwise the fish will curl up. Use a fish slice to press it down.

Cook the fish with the skin side down until it is about 80 per cent cooked. This should take about 3–4 minutes. Don't be afraid to turn the heat up or down to control the cooking. When the fish is mostly cooked, turn it and add in 1 tablespoon of butter, 200ml of fish stock and the fresh thyme. Finish the fish in this emulsion for 2–3 minutes. Now you are ready to serve.

To plate, place a good spoon of red pepper purée on the plate and swipe through it with a palette knife. Place some orzo to one side of the purée, then lay a piece of fish on top. Arrange the baby vegetables and glazed beetroot around the orzo. Finish with some spinach purée on the plate, if using, and serve.

Venison and Barley Risotto

with Cavolo Nero

I find a lot of people won't try venison as they reckon it will have a very strong flavour, when in fact it is the most mild of all the game meats. A lot of other people think the loin of venison is just as good as beef, if not better. This is an Irish take on a risotto that I learned in college, which cuts out the time-consuming process of stirring stock into risotto rice.

SERVES 4

INGREDIENTS

4 portions of venison loin, about 200g each
400g pearl barley
Sea salt to season
3 tablespoons spinach purée (see page 177), plus extra for serving
Cracked black pepper to season
Olive oil
2 tablespoons dried cranberries, chopped
4–5 long leaves of cavolo nero, stem removed and cut into quarters
1 teaspoon butter

TO GARNISH

Celeriac purée (see page 175)
Red wine jus made with cherry balsamic vinegar (see page 183)

METHOD

Leave the venison out at room temperature for 30 minutes before cooking.

Cover the pearl barley with water and boil it for 25–30 minutes until soft and tender. Season with sea salt and then stir the spinach purée through it. Set aside to reheat when serving.

Preheat the oven to 190°C/410°F/gas mark 6.

Season the venison nicely with sea salt and cracked black pepper. Heat a frying pan, pour in 2 tablespoons of olive oil and seal the venison all around. Once sealed, transfer it to an ovenproof dish, place in the preheated oven and cook to your liking. I normally like to cook mine medium rare to medium. This normally takes 4–5 minutes in the oven. Once cooked allow the venison to rest.

While the meat is resting you can prepare everything to serve. Reheat the barley risotto in a saucepan over a medium heat and add the chopped cranberries to it, mixing them through.

Sauté the cavolo nero in the butter and a splash of olive oil, and season with sea salt. This will take around 2–3 minutes.

To plate, spoon some celeriac purée and spinach purée onto the plate. Lay down the barley risotto in the middle. Slice the venison and lay it on top of the barley and then place the cavolo nero to the side. Serve with the red wine jus on the side.

Glazed Belly of Pork

with Truffle Risotto

A gorgeous main course to add to your repertoire. The truffle in the risotto is one of the greatest things in the world. And how could anyone say no to the glazed pork on top?

SERVES 4

INGREDIENTS

800g boneless pork belly, skin on

8 sprigs of fresh thyme

FOR THE RISOTTO

1 onion, diced

2 cloves of garlic, crushed

Olive oil

300g Arborio rice (risotto rice)

300ml white wine

1 litre chicken or vegetable stock

100ml cream

2 teaspoons butter

Sea salt to season

2g fresh truffle

FOR THE GLAZE

300ml honey

100ml balsamic vinegar

50ml soy sauce

TO SERVE

Spinach purée (see page 177)

10g affilla cress

METHOD

Preheat the oven to 150°C/325°F/gas mark 3.

Place the pork belly into a braising dish, scatter with the thyme and fill the dish with water until it covers the pork. Now cover it tightly with tinfoil and place into the oven to cook slowly for 3–4 hours. I highly recommend cooking the pork the day before.

Remove the pork carefully from the braising juices (reserve to use as a stock for soup). Remove the skin. Place the cooked pork on a baking sheet lined with cling film, then place another baking sheet on top with something on top to weigh it down. This will give the pork a firm, even shape. Allow to cool and set in the fridge for at least 3 hours, or preferably overnight.

In a large, wide saucepan, sweat the onion and garlic in some olive oil on a medium heat until soft. Turn down the heat to low and add the rice. Pour in the white wine and, keeping the heat low, allow to reduce by more than half. Heat the stock in another saucepan.

Keeping the rice on a low heat, add 2 small ladlefuls of stock to the rice and stir every now

and again to stop it from sticking. Add in a ladle-ful of stock every time the liquid reduces on the rice and continue stirring until the small white grain in the centre of the rice has disappeared and you've used all the stock.

Stir in the cream and butter and cook for 1–2 minutes, stirring constantly. Finally, season to taste and finely grate in the tiniest amount of fresh truffle.

Make the glaze by placing all the ingredients into a saucepan and bringing them to the boil. Be careful it doesn't overflow. Cut the pork into nice portions, 2 per person, and lay them into the glaze for 4–5 minutes on a medium simmer to heat through and become sticky.

To plate, make a splash of spinach purée on the plate, then spoon the risotto to the side. Lay the glazed pork belly on top of the risotto, top with some shavings of leftover truffle and finally add a little affilla cress.

Pork Fillet Wrapped in Prosciutto

It is very easy to overcook a fillet of pork. So this recipe is all about getting your timings right. The salty prosciutto on the outside of the pork works amazingly with the pesto.

SERVES 2

INGREDIENTS

350g pork fillet, well trimmed

2–3 tablespoons basil pesto

4–6 slices of prosciutto ham

Olive oil

4 pork and leek sausages

2 teaspoons butter

1 head of little gem lettuce, sliced thinly

TO SERVE

2 tablespoons carrot and star anise purée (see page 176)

2 tablespoons apple purée (see page 176)

Red wine jus (see page 183)

METHOD

Smear the outside of the pork fillet all over with the pesto. Lay a double layer of cling film on your work surface and place the slices of prosciutto on the cling film with the edges overlapping slightly. Place the pork fillet on the middle of the prosciutto and then wrap the prosciutto over the pork using the cling film. Once rolled up, secure the pork fillet by squeezing shut the ends of the cling film and roll into a large perfect sausage shape. Chill for 2–3 hours. Once chilled, slice into 2 portions. Carefully remove the cling film.

Preheat the oven to 180°C/400°F/gas mark 6.

Heat a large, ovenproof frying pan on a medium heat and add some olive oil. Add the pork fillet portions and cook for 2–3 minutes until golden, sealing on all sides. Transfer to a plate.

Add the sausages to the same pan and cook for 5 minutes, until lightly golden, then return the pork fillet to the pan and transfer to the oven. Roast for 8–10 minutes, until the pork portions are cooked through and the sausages are tender and golden brown.

Remove from the oven and leave to rest for 5 minutes in a warm place, then trim off the ends of the sausages to neaten.

Melt the butter in a saucepan with 2 tablespoons of olive oil and sauté the little gem until softened on a high heat. This will take about 2–3 minutes.

To plate, squeeze the apple and carrot purées beside each other from a squeezy bottle onto the plate. Lay the little gem in the middle of the plate. Slice the pork fillet and lay it on top. Add the sausage and then finish with 2 spoonfuls of red wine jus over the pork.

Halibut

with Chorizo, Mussels and Girolle Mushrooms

This delicate fish has a lovely summery feel. It a great one to start on if you are new to cooking fish. It is light, has a nice colour and can be the most flavoursome thing in the world.

SERVES 4

INGREDIENTS

Olive oil

4 halibut fillets (about 150g each), skinned and
    pin-boned

Sea salt to season

Butter

300ml fish stock (see page 179)

100g chorizo, peeled and diced

2 baby fennel bulbs, trimmed and quartered

11–12 girolle mushroom stalks, trimmed and
    brushed clean with a damp pastry brush

25–30 mussels, scrubbed

300ml white wine

Zest and juice of ½ lemon

200g spinach

FOR THE CANDIED LEMON SLICES

1 large unwaxed lemon, scrubbed

130g sugar

300ml water

TO SERVE

A handful of picked tops of dill

METHOD

First prepare the candied lemon slices. Cut the ends off the lemon and slice as thinly as possible, using a sharp knife or a mandoline. Boil the sugar in the water in a saucepan for 5 minutes. Drop in the lemon slices and simmer for 3–4 minutes, then take the pan off the heat. Leave the lemons to steep in the syrup overnight.

Heat some olive oil in a large frying pan until you can feel the heat rising. Season the halibut fillets with sea salt and fry on the presentation side, without moving, for about 2–3 minutes on a high heat until nice and golden brown. Add a tablespoon of butter and turn the fillets over carefully with a fish slice. Splash in the fish stock and cook for another 30 seconds to 1 minute, basting the fish with the pan juices. The fillets should feel slightly springy when pressed. Set aside to rest for 2 minutes.

While the fish is cooking you can also be cooking the chorizo. In a separate frying pan with a lid, on a medium heat, fry off the chorizo until golden and crispy. It doesn't need any oil as it will release its own. Drain on some kitchen paper and clean the pan.

Add some olive oil to the chorizo pan and fry off the baby fennel quarters and girolle mushrooms on a high heat until you get a nice colour and they soften.

Add the mussels to the pan with the fennel, then add the white wine and put the lid on. Cook the mussels, shaking now and again, for 2–3 minutes or until they open. Once cooked, remove the lid, add a tablespoon of butter and finish with the lemon zest and juice. Taste the liquid and season if needed. Cook the sauce without the lid for 1–2 minutes. The sauce should be buttery and reduced nicely at this stage.

Cook the spinach for 30 seconds to 1 minute in some olive oil and 1 teaspoon of butter on a high heat until wilted. Season with sea salt and drain on some kitchen paper in a bowl.

To plate, start with a spoon of spinach in the centre of the plate. Lay the halibut on top. Top the halibut with a slice of candied lemon. Spoon the fennel, girolles, mussels, crispy chorizo and finally some of the sauce from the mussels around the plate. Finish with the dill as a garnish.

DESSERT

Individual Lemon Meringue Tarts

A showstopper dessert to land on the table at any dinner party. Have these made just before dinner and store them in the fridge until ready to serve. I like to do my meringue in front of everyone with a blowtorch as it adds such a 'wow' factor.

MAKES 6

INGREDIENTS

FOR THE SHORTCRUST PASTRY
225g plain flour, plus extra for dusting
Pinch of caster sugar
100g butter, cubed, at room temperature
Zest of 1 lemon (optional)
2 tablespoons milk

FOR THE LEMON CURD
3 lemons
3 eggs
Seeds from ½ vanilla pod
50g butter
100g caster sugar
1 teaspoon cornflour

FOR THE MERINGUE
120g egg white (approx. 4 large egg whites)
150g caster sugar

METHOD
Try to be confident and bring the pastry together as quickly as you can. Don't knead it too much or the heat from your hands will melt the butter. A good tip is to hold your hands under cold, running water beforehand to make them as cold as possible. That way you'll end up with a delicate, flaky pastry every time.

Sieve the flour from a height into a clean bowl and mix in the sugar. Using your hands, work the cubes of butter into the flour and sugar by rubbing your thumbs against your fingers until you end up with a fine, crumbly mixture. This is the point where you can spike the mixture with interesting flavours, so mix in your lemon zest if using.

If the pastry is too dry, add the milk to the mixture and gently work it together until you have a ball of dough. Flour it lightly. Don't work the pastry too much at this stage or it will become elastic and chewy, not crumbly and short. Flour your work surface and place the dough on top. Pat it into a flat round, flour it again, lightly, and wrap it in cling film. Put it into the fridge to rest for at least half an hour.

While the pastry is chilling, make the lemon curd. Zest and juice the three lemons and then place all the curd ingredients into a bowl and set over a pot of simmering water. This is called a bain-marie. Whisk it all together and you'll notice the mixture will thicken after 15–20 minutes. Once thickened, you can pass it through a sieve to make it smooth. The easiest and fastest way to do this is to use a ladle to push it through the sieve.

Preheat the oven to 180°C/400°F/gas mark 6.

Roll the pastry nice and thin, then line six 10cm loose-bottomed tart tins with it. Line the pastry with some scrunched-up parchment paper or some heatproof cling film, then fill it with either baking beans, rice or dried marrowfat peas. A top tip is to fill each one to the brim, otherwise the sides will shrink. Bake the pastry blind for 10 minutes.

Remove from the oven and take out the lining and whatever else you have used, then bake for a further 10 minutes in the oven until crispy. Take them out and allow to cool. Once the pastry is cooled, add 2 tablespoons of the curd filling and place into the fridge to set the curd for 15–20 minutes.

Once you've that done you can make the meringue. In a clean, dry bowl whisk the egg white with an electric mixer until stiff peaks form. You should be able to hold this upside down over your head without it dropping. If it is too loose keep whisking until you achieve this. If the egg white is under-whisked it will turn into a sloppy mixture.

Add the sugar, in small amounts at a time, continuing to whisk until it is all used. If you add all the sugar in at once the meringue won't hold its stiff peaks. Once ready, spread the meringue on top of the curd with a spatula or you can even go to the effort of piping it on with a nozzle if you want this to look really impressive.

To finish you can blowtorch the meringue or pop the tarts under the grill for 1–2 minutes to colour nicely. Place into the fridge until ready to serve.

Vanilla Crème Brûlée

The traditional recipe for crème brûlée is made with double cream and is rich and delicious. This version of the classic French dinner-party dessert uses milk instead of double cream. It tastes just as good but is much lighter. For a bit of variety you can put a layer of stewed fruit in the bottom, such as raspberries or apple. This dish can be prepared 3 or 4 hours in advance.

**MAKES 4 X 10CM RAMEKINS
OR 2 LARGE BRÛLÉE DISHES**

INGREDIENTS

300ml whole milk

1 vanilla pod

4 egg yolks

40g caster sugar

40g demerara sugar

METHOD

Put the milk in a saucepan. Then, with a small, sharp knife, split the vanilla pod lengthways and, using the back of the blade, scrape all the seeds from inside the pod into the milk. Chop the pod finely and add to the saucepan. Bring the milk to the boil, then cook at a gentle simmer for 5 minutes. Turn off the heat and set aside.

Put the egg yolks and caster sugar in a mixing bowl and whisk together until a pale straw colour. Pour the hot milk onto the egg yolk mixture. Mix well, then strain the milk and egg yolk mixture through a fine sieve into a clean pan, pressing on the vanilla pods and seeds to extract as much flavour as possible. Spoon off any foam from the surface, then set aside.

Preheat the oven to 140°C/320°F/gas mark 3.

Pour equal quantities of the mixture into the ramekins or brûlée dishes. Line a deep roasting tin or dish just large enough to hold the ramekins/dishes with kitchen paper. Place the filled ramekins/dishes into this, on top of the paper (during cooking the kitchen paper serves as a form of insulation against the strong heat

from the oven and prevents the brûlée from overcooking). Add enough boiling water to the tin or dish to reach three-quarters of the height of the ramekins/dishes. Transfer the tin to the oven and bake for about 30–40 minutes until the mixture has just set.

When the mixture has set, remove each ramekin/dish from the water and leave to cool at room temperature. When cold, chill for at least 1 hour. An easy way of checking if the brûlée is set is by hitting the side of the roasting dish. If they have a slight wobble, then you know they are ready.

Sprinkle equal amounts of the demerara sugar over the brûlées, then either blowtorch the sugar or place them under the grill. If the latter, preheat the grill until it is very hot. Caramelise under the grill for 2–3 minutes according to its strength.

Leave to cool and set into a delightful layer of crisp caramel. When set, place the dishes on serving plates with doilies and serve. Don't be afraid to scoop some ice cream on top!

Caramelised Calvados Apples

and Granny Smith Purée with Vanilla Ice Cream and a Filo Triangle

This is a really simple dish to put together. If you want, you can have everything made a day in advance and then all you need to do is reheat the apples on a medium heat in a small saucepan.

SERVES 4

INGREDIENTS

2 large Braeburn apples

½ lemon (optional)

100g caster sugar

50g butter

4 tablespoons Calvados apple brandy

FOR THE FILO TRIANGLE

1 sheet of filo pastry

10g melted butter

2 tablespoons caster sugar

½ teaspoon ground cinnamon

TO SERVE

40g Granny Smith apple purée (see page 176)

4 scoops of vanilla ice cream (see page 186)

METHOD

Start by peeling and coring the apples. Cut them in half, then in quarters and finally cut each quarter into half. You should be left with eight wedges per apple. If you are afraid of the apples going brown, squeeze some lemon juice over them.

Add the sugar and butter to a large frying pan on a high heat. Allow them to dissolve and colour on the high heat until you reach a toffee colour you are happy with. Do not be tempted to stir the caramel at any stage as it will split and you'll have to start again. Just lightly swirl it every now and again. Remember caramel becomes extremely hot, so be very careful.

Once the caramel has reached a toffee colour, add the apple wedges to the pan. Reduce the heat to low and colour the apples on each side. This takes about 2–3 minutes. When you are happy with the colour of the apples, add the Calvados to flambé. To do this you can either tip the pan over your gas flame, or light a match over the pan. This basically cooks off the alcohol and gives a delicious musty sweet flavour.

Once flambéed, place the apples and caramel onto a steel tray and allow to cool as quickly as they can, so they don't overcook. Reheat in a saucepan over a medium heat before serving.

Preheat the oven to 180°C/400°F/gas mark 6.

For the filo triangle garnish you have to work fast or else the filo pastry will dry out. First, cut the filo pastry right down the middle. Now, starting at the corner, with your knife cut out a nice 45-degree triangle. Repeat, cutting out triangles all along the filo sheet until you've used it all up. You may have too many, but it's always good to have extras as they can break fairly easily.

You'll need two flat trays that are the same size. Brush each triangle with melted butter and then lay them all onto a sheet of parchment paper on top of one of the trays. Mix the sugar and cinnamon in a bowl and then sprinkle from a height over the filo pastry. Lay another sheet of parchment paper on top and place the other tray on top of this, so they don't curl up while cooking.

Bake for 12–15 minutes until golden and crisp, then set aside until serving. I normally keep mine in an airtight container until I need them.

To serve, arrange four apple wedges in the bottom of a nice bowl with some of the Calvados caramel. Next squeeze some dots of the Granny Smith purée around the apples. Lay a scoop of ice cream on top and then finally top with the crispy filo triangle.

Panna Cotta

with Mixed Berry Compote

If you are only starting out cooking and hosting for guests, panna cotta is a great dessert to start with. It is very simple to put together and easy to serve on the day. Try to use in-season berries for the compote.

SERVES 6

INGREDIENTS

4 gelatine leaves

500ml double cream

100ml coconut milk

100g caster sugar

Seeds from 1 vanilla pod

FOR THE BERRY COMPOTE

3 tablespoons red wine

2 tablespoons crème de cassis

50g caster sugar

1 cinnamon stick

1 whole star anise

Seeds from ½ vanilla pod

100g mixed, in-season berries (such as blackberries, blueberries, raspberries and strawberries)

TO SERVE

6 sprigs of mint

METHOD

To make the panna cotta, put the gelatine leaves in a bowl of cold water and leave to soak for 10 minutes. Put the cream, coconut milk, sugar and vanilla seeds into a small saucepan and slowly bring to the boil. Take the saucepan off the heat, gently squeeze the soaked gelatine leaves dry and add them to the pan, whisking continuously until they have dissolved. Strain the mixture through a sieve into a measuring jug, which makes it easy to pour. Allow to cool completely.

Once the panna cotta mixture is cool, give it a good stir to disperse the vanilla seeds so they don't all float to the bottom of the moulds. Then divide the mixture equally between six 150ml (¼ pint) dariole moulds and leave them to set in the fridge for at least 3 hours and up to 2 days.

Prepare the berry compote. Place the red wine, crème de cassis, sugar, cinnamon, star anise and vanilla seeds in a small saucepan with a lid. Cook on a medium heat for 5–10 minutes until syrupy. Stir in the berries. Cover the pan with the lid, remove from the heat and allow the berries and syrup to cool completely. You'll notice the berries will soften in the heat of the liquid.

To serve, unmould the panna cotta by dipping briefly into hot water, then place a plate face down on top of each mould and flip, allowing them to drop out on their own. Spoon some berry compote around the edge and decorate with a mint sprig.

Pear Tart Tatin

This elegant dessert is designed to serve two, but you can easily make an extra tatin or two to serve more. I find vanilla pods dusted with icing sugar are the perfect finishing touch. Dry the empty pods after you have used them in the ice cream to use for decoration.

SERVES 2

INGREDIENTS

4 large ripe pears (any kind)
250g ready-made puff pastry
50g cold, unsalted butter
50g caster sugar

TO SERVE

2–3 vanilla pods (seeds removed), sliced
    lengthways and dusted with icing sugar
    (optional)
Vanilla ice cream (see page 186)

METHOD

Peel and halve the pears, then scoop out the cores using a melon baller. Lay the pears out on a tray lined with kitchen paper and pat them with more kitchen paper. Leave to dry uncovered for a few hours, or chill overnight if possible – it won't matter if they discolour because they will be coated in caramel.

Roll out the puff pastry thinly on a lightly floured surface and cut out a 24cm round, using a similar-sized plate as a guide. Lift onto a baking sheet and chill while you prepare the filling.

Cut the butter into thin slices and scatter over the bottom of a 20cm, shallow, ovenproof pan. Sprinkle over the sugar. Arrange the pear halves neatly around the pan with one in the middle. Place over a medium heat until the butter and sugar have melted and formed a light caramel. Carefully shake the pan every now and again to ensure that the pears are well coated with the caramel and are evenly brown. Leave to cool slightly.

When ready to cook, preheat the oven to 200°C/425°F/gas mark 7. Drape the pastry over the pears and carefully tuck the edges down the side of the pan. Place the pan into the hot oven and bake for 15 minutes. Lower the oven setting to 180°C/400°F/gas mark 6 and bake for a further 10–15 minutes until the pastry is golden brown and crisp. Leave to cool.

To serve, dust the vanilla pods (if using) heavily with icing sugar, shaking off the excess. Turn out the tart tatin onto a serving plate, top with the sugar-dusted vanilla pods and serve with scoops of vanilla ice cream in small bowls on the side.

Rice Pudding Soufflé

with Passion Fruit Sorbet

A soufflé never fails to impress. Just make sure you have everything ready and waiting the moment you take the dishes from the oven – serving plates, sorbet and guests. Make the soufflé base well in advance, but be ready to whip up the meringue and fold it into the soufflé base at the last minute.

SERVES 4

INGREDIENTS

50g unsalted butter, plus extra for greasing

110g pudding rice

520g full-fat milk

520g double cream

1 vanilla pod (split in half lengthways)

270g caster sugar, plus extra for coating the dishes

Pinch of sea salt

Butter for greasing

400g egg white

TO SERVE

100ml dark chocolate, melted

Passion fruit sorbet (see page 185)

METHOD

Preheat the oven to 120°C/275°F/gas mark 1.

Melt the butter in an ovenproof pan, add the pudding rice and fry gently for 3 minutes. Add the milk, cream, vanilla pod, 110g of caster sugar and a pinch of sea salt. Bring to the boil, then turn down the heat and simmer, stirring frequently, for 20 minutes or until the mix is thick.

Cover with a lid and bake the rice in the oven for an hour, stirring every 20 minutes until the mixture has thickened even more. Remove the rice from the oven, transfer to a blender, making sure to remove the vanilla pod, and blend to a smooth purée. You can make this base well in advance so you are prepared.

About 45 minutes before serving, warm up 500g of the soufflé base by placing it in a bowl in a large pan half-filled with warm water for about 20–25 minutes; this will make it easier to work with.

While the base is reheating, preheat the oven to 190°C/410°F/gas mark 6.

Brush four 300ml individual soufflé dishes with soft butter. Chill until firm, then brush again with another layer of butter. Dip into a bowl of caster sugar, shake the sugar around the ramekins so that they are evenly coated, then tip out any excess.

Whisk the egg white in a clean, dry bowl until stiff, then whisk in 160g of caster sugar a tablespoon at a time until fully incorporated and the meringue still holds a peak.

When the soufflé base is reheated, fold the meringue gently into it using a large metal spoon. Spoon the soufflé mixture into the moulds and level off the tops with a palette knife. Run your thumb along the edge of each mould: this gives them an extra lift.

Bake the soufflés for about 10–14 minutes. They are ready when they are golden brown and feel a little springy when lightly pressed.

While the soufflé is cooking, pipe some melted chocolate onto the serving plates. Spoon the sorbet on the side just before they are cooked and then stand a soufflé dish on each serving plate.

Chocolate and Hazelnut Tart

Also known as death by chocolate, this tart always reminds me of Ferrero Rocher. I love the simplicity of a tart where you can surprise people with the different flavours in the mixture.

SERVES 6

INGREDIENTS

FOR THE CHOCOLATE TUILES
2 eggs whites
90g caster sugar
55g plain flour
1 level teaspoon cocoa powder
55g unsalted butter, melted and cooled

FOR THE SHORTCRUST PASTRY
225g plain flour, plus a little extra for dusting
Pinch of caster sugar
100g butter, cubed, at room temperature
1–2 tablespoons milk

FOR THE CHOCOLATE TART MIX
50g toasted hazelnuts
450g dark chocolate, broken into small pieces
1 teaspoon cocoa powder
4 eggs
85g caster sugar
230ml cream
120ml milk

TO SERVE
Chocolate and hazelnut ice cream (see page 187)

METHOD

You can make the tuiles a day or two in advance. Line a baking tray with a silicone liner. Put the egg whites and sugar in a bowl and lightly beat with a fork. Sift in the flour with the cocoa powder and stir to mix well. Add the butter and stir until evenly blended.

Using a palette knife, spread a few thin strips of the tuile mix on the liner. Bake for 7–8 minutes until they are brown around the edges with a matt appearance. Leave to cool for a minute or two. While they are still pliable, lift each tuile with a palette knife and twist to resemble a pair of wings. Leave to cool and set. They will become crisp and brittle. Use all the mixture to make extras as these break really easily. The mixture normally makes ten to fifteen. Store in an airtight container until ready to serve.

When making the pastry, try to be confident and bring it together as quickly as you can. Don't knead it too much or the heat from your hands will melt the butter. A good tip is to hold your hands under cold, running water beforehand to make them as cold as possible. That way you'll end up with a delicate, flaky pastry every time.

Sieve the flour from a height into a clean bowl and mix the sugar with it. Using your hands, work the cubes of butter into the flour and sugar by rubbing your thumbs against your fingers until you end up with a fine, crumbly mixture.

If the pastry is too dry, add the milk to the mixture and gently work it together until you have a ball of dough. Flour it lightly. Don't work the pastry too much at this stage or it will become elastic and chewy, not crumbly and short. Flour your work surface and place the dough on top. Pat it into a flat round, flour it again, lightly, and wrap it in cling film. Put it into the fridge to rest for at least half an hour.

Preheat the oven to 180°C/400°F/gas mark 6.

Roll out the pastry and line six mini loose-bottomed tart tins with it, then line the pastry with some scrunched-up parchment paper or heatproof cling film. Fill with either baking beans, rice or dried marrowfat peas. A top tip is to fill the pastry to the brim, otherwise the sides will shrink. Bake the pastry blind for 10 minutes, then remove from the oven and take out whatever you used to line it during blind baking. Return the tartlet tins to the oven and bake the pastry for a further 5–10 minutes in the oven until crispy. Take out and allow to cool.

For the chocolate filling, start by pulsing the hazelnuts in a food processor until they are coarsely chopped. Place the chocolate, cocoa powder, eggs and sugar in a bowl.

Boil the cream and milk together. Pour the hot milk–cream mix over the chocolate mix and whisk until smooth, then pass through a sieve. Once sieved, add in most of the hazelnuts – keep a small amount back for decoration.

Pour this mixture into the pastry cases and bake at 90°C/225°F/gas mark ¼ for 30–40 minutes, or until there's a slight wobble in the centre. Leave to cool, then place into the fridge until ready to serve.

To serve, set an individual tart on a plate and top with a sprinkle of toasted hazelnuts and a tuile. To finish, add a neat scoop of chocolate and hazelnut ice cream to the side.

Tiramisu

This is my twist on the classic tiramisu. I love serving food in martini glasses. It makes it look so elegant.

SERVES 4

INGREDIENTS

100ml espresso (or strong instant) coffee

2 tablespoons coffee liqueur

4 Savoiardi biscuits

2 large egg whites

250g mascarpone cheese

2 tablespoons honey

2 tablespoons Marsala

TO SERVE

2 teaspoons good-quality cocoa powder

METHOD

Make your espresso and pour it into a heatproof jug, then add the coffee liqueur and leave it to cool.

Break a Savoiardi sponge finger into about four and drop the pieces into a martini glass, then pour some of the cooled espresso mixture over the pieces. Push them down gently, making sure the biscuits are soaked all over. Repeat in three more glasses.

Using a hand-held electric whisk, beat the egg whites until they form soft peaks, then set aside.

Scrape the mascarpone into another bowl and add the honey. Beat with the whisk (no need to clean it first) and, when smooth, slowly beat in the Marsala.

Fold in the egg whites, a third at a time, with a spatula, then dollop this mixture over the soused Savoiardi in each glass. Using a palette knife, smooth off the top.

Let these stand in the fridge for at least 20 minutes and up to 24 hours, then dust with cocoa powder, pushing it through a sieve, just before serving.

Lemon Posset

with Marinated Berries

A gorgeously light dessert which goes down easy after a heavy, hearty meal. It really can refresh your palate.

SERVES 4–6

INGREDIENTS

600ml cream

150g caster sugar

1 vanilla pod

Juice and zest of 1 lemon

1 large passion fruit

FOR THE MARINATED BERRIES

2 tablespoons crème de cassis

1 teaspoon blackberry balsamic vinegar (or
    ordinary balsamic)

1 teaspoon vanilla extract

250g mixed strawberries and raspberries

TO SERVE

4–6 mint sprigs

METHOD

Start by placing the cream in a pan with the sugar, vanilla pod and lemon zest and juice. Cut the passion fruit in half, scoop out the seeds and pulp, and pass them through a sieve. Add the passion fruit juice to the pan. Bring to the boil and boil for 1–2 minutes.

Leave the mixture to cool slightly. Have a taste just to make sure that the mixture isn't too bitter. You can adjust the bitterness by adding extra sugar at this stage. Pass the mixture through a sieve to remove any bits and the vanilla pod. Pour into 4–6 glasses (tumblers), depending on their size.

Chill for at least 1–2 hours, but overnight is best.

Pour the crème de cassis, blackberry balsamic vinegar and vanilla extract over the mixed berries in a container or bowl. Cover with cling film and shake. Leave for 1–2 hours, or overnight if possible, to infuse.

To plate, place the posset-filled glasses on a serving plate, spoon over some of the marinated berries and top with a mint sprig.

Red Wine Poached Pears

Such a simple, elegant-looking dessert loved by all. Choose a good-quality red wine – one you'd like to drink – as it will flavour the pears nicely. With the juices that are left over, you can make a nice gel.

SERVES 4

INGREDIENTS

1 bottle good-quality red wine

2 tablespoons lemon juice

1 teaspoon vanilla extract

1 cinnamon stick

60g caster sugar (you may need more depending on the wine you use)

1 star anise

4 pears

TO SERVE

Poached pear gel (see page 184)

4 spun sugar nests (see page 184)

Some of the poaching liquid from the pears

METHOD

To a saucepan that's big enough for poaching pears (it should fit all the pears comfortably), add the red wine, lemon juice, vanilla extract, cinnamon, sugar and star anise. Stir over a high heat until the sugar dissolves, bring to the boil and then reduce the heat to medium to low so it stays on a steady simmer.

Meanwhile prepare the pears by scooping out the bottom of them with a small melon baller. A small tomato knife will do the same job. Don't use an apple corer, as you will lose the stem at the top.

Carefully peel the pears with a speed peeler, then place them gently into the poaching liquid lying on their sides. Allow them to simmer untouched for 12–14 minutes without a lid so the liquid can reduce and thicken to a syrup.

Turn the pears over and poach them on the other side for a further 8–10 minutes. Check the base of the pears with a fork, you are looking for them to be nice and tender, but not too soft, or they will fall apart.

Remove the pears from the poaching liquid carefully and allow to cool. Pass the poaching liquid through a sieve and set aside half of it for the gel and the other half for serving.

Make the poached pear gel.

To plate, I normally use small serving plates. Squeeze a nice design onto the plate with the gel, and in the middle of it stand the poached pear up carefully. Lay a spun sugar nest on top. Serve some of the poaching liquid on the side so the guests can pour it over themselves.

PETIT FOURS

Madeleines

These French classics are best served with a cup of tea or coffee. Madeleines don't keep very well so they are best served on the day. However, the raw mixture will keep in the fridge for up to a week and you can simply cook them fresh on the day.

MAKES 25–30

INGREDIENTS

160g butter, plus extra melted for greasing
50g plain flour, plus extra for dusting
5 egg whites at room temperature
160g icing sugar
70g ground almonds
40g toasted flaked almonds

METHOD

Lightly grease enough small madeleine tins for 25–30 buns with melted butter, then dust with flour, shaking off any excess. Place in the fridge for at least 2 hours, but overnight is best.

Preheat the oven to 190°C/410°F/gas mark 6.

Place the butter in a small pan and allow to brown slightly. Remove from the heat and leave to cool.

Sift the flour into a large bowl. Add the egg whites, icing sugar and ground almonds. Using an electric mixer, beat until well combined and smooth.

Slowly add the melted brown butter and mix gently for 5 minutes, until smooth and thickened.

Spoon the mixture into the prepared tins, so that it is about level with the top, leaving a little room for rising, then sprinkle over the toasted flaked almonds.

Bake for 10–12 minutes until well risen, golden and springy to the touch. Remove from the oven and leave to rest in the tins for 2 minutes, then ease out of the tins with a palette knife and leave to cool slightly on a wire rack before serving.

Coconut Chocolate Truffles

A delicious mouthful of creamy coconut goodness. You can have these made well in advance and stored in the fridge.

MAKES 25–30

INGREDIENTS

250g desiccated coconut, plus extra for
     dusting
300g condensed milk
150g dark chocolate (55% cocoa)
200g butter

METHOD

Roast the coconut in a tray in the oven at 180°C/400°F/gas mark 6 for 3–5 minutes, keeping an eye on it to make sure that it doesn't burn and stirring occasionally. Remove from the oven and allow to cool.

Pour the condensed milk into a mixing bowl. Melt the chocolate and butter together over a bain-marie of water, or in a bowl in the microwave with 3 x 30 second blasts, stirring in-between.

Once the chocolate and butter are melted, stir into the condensed milk with a spatula. Stir in the roasted coconut until it is well combined and place in a piping bag with a medium-sized nozzle or, alternatively, in a freezer bag with the corner cut off with scissors.

Line 2 baking trays with cling film and pipe out your preferred truffle size (I normally do half the size of a ping pong ball). Don't panic – they won't be a perfect shape at this stage.

Once you have the mixture piped out, place it into the freezer for an hour to chill and harden. Once they have hardened, roll them in your hands until you get a perfect round ball shape.

Once shaped, you can dust these in the extra coconut and keep in the fridge until you are ready to serve them. These are best served with a cup of tea or coffee.

Chocolate Macarons

Be sure to weigh the ingredients precisely for these elegant little things. These French delights are light, airy and meringue-like.

MAKES 25–30

FOR THE MACARONS

200g icing sugar

120g ground almonds

3 tablespoons cocoa powder

¼ teaspoon fine salt

3 large egg whites, at room temperature

¼ teaspoon cream of tartar

3 tablespoons granulated sugar

FOR THE GANACHE FILLING

120g dark chocolate (50% cocoa), finely
    chopped

120ml cream

25g unsalted butter, at room temperature
    and cut into cubes

METHOD

Line two baking sheets with parchment paper and set aside. Fit a large piping bag with a ½-inch plain nozzle and set aside.

Place the icing sugar, ground almonds, cocoa powder and salt in a food processor fitted with a blade attachment, and pulse several times to aerate. Process until fine and combined – about 30 seconds. Sift into a large bowl and set aside.

Make the meringue by placing the egg whites in the clean bowl of a stand mixer fitted with a whisk attachment; alternatively you can use a hand-held whisk and a bit of elbow grease. Beat on a medium speed until opaque and foamy – about 30 seconds. Add the cream of tartar, increase the speed to medium-high, and beat until the egg whites are white in colour and hold the line of the whisk – about 1 minute. Continue to beat, slowly adding the granulated sugar, until the sugar is combined, the peaks are stiff and the whites are shiny – about 1 minute more. (Try not to over-whip.) Transfer the meringue to a large bowl.

Using a rubber spatula, gently fold the dry mixture into the egg whites in four batches until the dry ingredients are just combined. The meringue will deflate so don't panic, but you don't want to over-mix this, so be gentle. After the final addition, stop folding when there are no traces of egg white and it looks like cake batter.

Transfer the batter to the piping bag. Pipe 3cm rounds about 3cm apart on the baking sheets, 25–30 per sheet. Pick up the baking sheets and bang them against the work surface to help create the macaron base. Let the rounds sit at room temperature for 30 minutes to dry the tops and ensure even cooking.

Heat the oven to 180°C/400°F/gas mark 6 and arrange a rack in the middle. Bake one sheet of the macarons for 7 minutes. Rotate the sheet and cook for 7 minutes more. Transfer the sheet to a rack to cool completely. Repeat with the second baking sheet.

To make the ganache, place the chopped chocolate in a large bowl. Warm the cream in a small saucepan over a medium heat until it just starts to boil. Stir it into the chocolate without creating bubbles. Let sit for 1 minute. Add the butter and stir until smooth. Chill in the fridge until thickened but still spreadable. This should take about 30 minutes.

Once the macarons and ganache are cool, pair macarons of similar size. Remove the ganache from the fridge. If you choose to pipe the ganache, transfer it to a disposable piping bag and snip about half an inch off the bottom. Squeeze or scoop the ganache to about the size of a cherry (about 1 teaspoon) onto the centre of a macaron half. Top with the other half and press gently so that it looks like a mini hamburger. The filling should not ooze out the edges.

Refrigerate, covered, for at least 24 hours before serving.

Irish Cream Liqueur Truffles

I can remember rolling hundreds of these in my first job as a commis chef. The Irish cream liqueur and white chocolate are a match made in heaven.

MAKES 25–35

INGREDIENTS
150ml cream
400g white chocolate, melted
2 tablespoons Irish cream liqueur
Cocoa powder, for coating

METHOD
Pour the cream into a saucepan and bring it to the boil, then pour it over the melted chocolate. Stir until it's combined, then stir in the Irish cream liqueur – a spatula is a good way to ensure it is really well combined.

Leave the mixture to cool, then chill for at least 4–5 hours, or preferably overnight.

Scoop the mixture out using a melon baller or teaspoon and roll into round balls. Drop the balls into some cocoa powder and roll them around to coat them, then lift them out of the cocoa powder, shaking off any excess.

Place the truffles in a container lined with parchment paper and keep refrigerated until serving.

Simple Fudge

Please don't hyperventilate at the amount of sugar in this recipe – it makes an awful lot of fudge. You can cut the recipe in half if you like.

MAKES AROUND 60–70 PIECES

INGREDIENTS
250g soft butter
397g tin of condensed milk
175ml whole milk
2 tablespoons golden syrup
800g granulated sugar
2 teaspoons vanilla extract

METHOD
Grease a tin approximately 30 x 20cm.

Put all the ingredients, excluding the vanilla extract, into a large, heavy-bottomed pan and bring to the boil, stirring constantly.

Boil for 12–20 minutes with a sugar thermometer in, still stirring all the time, until the mixture is golden and reaches 116°C, also known as soft-ball stage. (Your sugar thermometer should have both these readings on it.) How long this takes depends on how ferociously the mixture bubbles, as well as on the properties and dimensions of the pan. This is hot caramel so please be careful.

When the fudge is at soft-ball stage, very carefully remove the pan from the stove and stir in the vanilla. Being careful not to let it splash you and, preferably using an electric whisk, beat for about five minutes, by which time the fudge will have thickened to the texture of stiff peanut butter. Pour and push into the prepared tin. Smooth the top as well as you can.

Put in the fridge to cool, but don't keep it there for more than 2 hours or it will set too hard. Remove from the fridge and, using a sharp knife, cut into small squares.

Jammy Dodgers

These are made using the classic French pâté sablée or 'sweet pastry', which is rich and buttery. The pastry is very short, so it is important to let it rest; this makes it easier to handle. Raspberry jam works well in these, but you can try other varieties too.

MAKES 6

INGREDIENTS
275g plain flour, plus extra for dusting
220g unsalted butter, diced
100g icing sugar, sifted
A pinch of salt
2 medium egg yolks
140g raspberry jam

METHOD
Place the flour, butter, icing sugar and salt in a mixing bowl. Rub together until the mixture resembles breadcrumbs. Add the egg yolks and bring together to form a ball.

On a lightly floured surface, knead gently to form a smooth ball of dough. Wrap this in cling film and place in the fridge for at least 30 minutes.

Line two baking trays with parchment paper.

On a lightly floured surface, roll out the dough to 0.5cm thick. Using a 9cm heart-shaped cutter, cut out twelve shapes. You will need to re-roll the trimmings to get twelve of these. Then, using a 4.5cm heart-shaped cutter, make a hole in the middle of six of the large biscuits.

Place the biscuits on the prepared trays and put into the fridge to rest for 30 minutes.

Preheat your oven to 170°C/375°F/gas mark 5.

Bake the biscuits for 12–14 minutes until pale and just beginning to colour, but cooked through. They should be a nice golden colour. The biscuits will be soft whilst warm, so leave on the trays for a few minutes until they have set, then transfer to a wire rack to cool.

Once cooled, take the whole biscuits and turn them upside down. Place a dollop of jam in the middle of each one. Spread it out a little, being careful not to go to the edges. Top each one with a biscuit with a hole in it and gently push together.

THE BASICS

This section has all the bits of mise en place which will allow you to be in control of your dinner party and ensure you keep your cool and don't get stressed. A lot of these recipes can be made 1–2 days in advance and stored until needed. The most organised kitchens I've worked in have all their preparation done in advance, ready to go for service.

Butternut Squash Purée

MAKES ABOUT 600ML

INGREDIENTS
1 small butternut squash, peeled and cubed
100g butter
Sea salt

METHOD
Place the butternut squash in a saucepan and cover with water. Boil until it is soft enough to mash with a fork.

Drain the water from the pan and allow the squash to steam so the water evaporates. You'll know the squash is ready to be blended when it starts to stick to the sides of the saucepan and no more steam rises from it.

Place the butter and softened squash into a blender. Season with sea salt and then blend until very smooth.

The purée should be a thick enough consistency to coat the back of a spoon. A good tip for stabilising a wet purée is to add a quarter teaspoon of xanthan gum to the purée and blitz until thickened.

If you like your purée very smooth, you can pass it through a sieve – use a ladle to push it through. (I highly recommend this if you plan to pipe the purée through a squeezy bottle.) This will keep for 3–4 days in the fridge.

Celeriac Purée

MAKES ABOUT 600ML

INGREDIENTS
1 celeriac, peeled and cubed
200ml cream
100g butter
Sea salt

METHOD
Place the celeriac in a saucepan and cover it with water. Boil it until it is soft enough to mash with a fork.

Drain off the water from the pan and allow the celeriac to steam so the water evaporates. Once it has stopped steaming, add the cream, bring to the boil and cook on a medium heat for 1 minute.

Place the celeriac, cream and butter into a blender. Season with sea salt, adding small amounts until you are happy with the taste, then blend until very smooth.

The purée should be a thick enough consistency to coat the back of a spoon. A good tip for stabilising a wet purée is to add a quarter teaspoon of xanthan gum to the purée and blitz until thickened.

If you like your purée very smooth, you can pass it through a sieve – use a ladle to push it through. (I highly recommend this if you plan to pipe the purée through a squeezy bottle.) This will keep for 3–4 days in the fridge.

Carrot and Star Anise Purée

MAKES ABOUT 600ML

INGREDIENTS

5 large carrots, peeled and sliced

2 star anise

200ml cream

100g butter

Sea salt

METHOD

Place the sliced carrot and star anise in a saucepan and cover with water. Boil until the carrots are very soft and can be mashed easily with a fork.

Drain the water from the pot and allow the carrot and star anise to steam so the water evaporates. Once it has stopped steaming, add the cream and place on a high heat. Bring to the boil, then turn down to a medium heat and cook for 1 minute.

Put the carrot, cream and butter into the blender. Discard the star anise before blending. Season with sea salt, adding small amounts until you are happy with the taste, then blend until very smooth.

The purée should be a thick enough consistency to coat the back of a spoon. A good tip for stabilising a wet purée is to add a quarter teaspoon of xanthan gum to the purée and blitz until thickened.

If you like your purée very smooth, you can pass it through a sieve – use a ladle to push it through. (I highly recommend this if you plan to pipe the purée through a squeezy bottle.) This will keep for 3–4 days in the fridge.

Granny Smith Apple Purée

MAKES ABOUT 600ML

INGREDIENTS

2 medium Granny Smith apples, peeled, cored and chopped

500ml water

250g sugar

Seeds from ½ vanilla pod

Green food colouring (optional)

METHOD

Put the apples, water, sugar and vanilla seeds in a saucepan and stew on a medium heat until the apples have softened and gone to mush.

Place the stewed apples into a food processor, add in a tiny drop of the food colouring if using and pulse until smooth. Place into a squeezy bottle until needed. This will keep in the fridge for up to a week.

Roasted Red Pepper Purée

MAKES ABOUT 600ML

INGREDIENTS
1 shallot diced
2 tablespoons olive oil
2 x 460g jars of roasted red peppers (or you can roast 2 red peppers)
3 tablespoons balsamic vinegar
1 tablespoon butter
Sea salt to season

METHOD
Sweat the shallot in the olive oil in a saucepan on a medium heat until softened.

Remove the peppers from the jars, draining off the brine. Chop roughly and then add to the saucepan with the shallot. Cook on a medium heat for 5 minutes, making sure to stir now and again.

Add the balsamic vinegar and cook for another 2–3 minutes.

Place the saucepan contents into a food processor and add the butter and a small amount of sea salt to taste. Blend until nice and smooth.

Pass through a fine sieve to make super smooth. Store in a squeezy bottle and use as required. This will keep for up to a week in the fridge.

Spinach Purée

MAKES ABOUT 400ML

INGREDIENTS
600g fresh spinach leaves, tough stalks removed
200ml cream
Sea salt to season

METHOD
Blanch the spinach for 1 minute in a pan of boiling salted water. Strain out the water, then pour in the cream and heat on low for 1 minute.

With a slotted spoon, add the wilted spinach to a food processor, reserving the cream to correct the consistency. Season with a small amount of sea salt to taste and pulse. Check the consistency and, if necessary, add small amounts of the cream you've reserved and pulse again to make the purée smoother.

Place in a squeezy bottle and use as required. This will keep for up to a week in the fridge.

Basil Purée

MAKES ABOUT 400ML

INGREDIENTS
600g fresh basil leaves, tough stalks removed
200ml cream
Sea salt to season

METHOD
Blanch the basil for 1 minute in a pan of boiling salted water. Strain out the water, then pour in the cream and heat on low for 1 minute.

With a slotted spoon, add the wilted basil to a food processor, reserving the cream to correct the consistency. Season with a small amount of sea salt to taste and pulse. Check the consistency and, if necessary, add small amounts of the cream you've reserved and pulse again to make the purée smoother.

Place in a squeezy bottle and use as required. This will keep for up to a week in the fridge.

Bacon and Onion Purée

MAKES ABOUT 300ML

INGREDIENTS
2 large onions, peeled and chopped
2 tablespoons olive oil
4 smoked streaky rashers, grilled and chopped
200ml cream
50g butter
Sea salt to season

METHOD
Fry the onions in the oil in a saucepan on a high heat until nicely coloured and golden. Add in the chopped rashers and cook for a further 1–2 minutes on a medium heat.

Now stir in the cream and bring to the boil. Reduce the cream down by half and then pop the contents of the pan into the blender. Add in a small amount of the butter and pulse. You may not need all the butter, so add in small amounts at a time until you get the consistency you want.

Check the seasoning and, if needed, add a little sea salt. For a smooth result pass the purée through a fine sieve. This can be stored for up to a week in the fridge.

Red Cabbage Purée

MAKES ABOUT 600ML

INGREDIENTS

300g red cabbage, finely chopped

2 tablespoons olive oil

800ml red wine

200ml balsamic vinegar

2–3 tablespoons butter

Sea salt to season

METHOD

In a saucepan with a lid, sweat the red cabbage in the oil until slightly softened. Add the red wine and balsamic vinegar and cook with the lid on over a medium heat for 40–50 minutes, until the cabbage is very soft.

Once the cabbage is cooked, remove the lid – the liquid should be well reduced.

Place the contents of the saucepan into the blender with 2 tablespoons of butter. Season with a small amount of sea salt to taste and pulse until smooth. If not smooth enough, add the other tablespoon of butter and pulse again.

Place in a squeezy bottle and use as required. This will keep for up to a week in the fridge.

Fish Stock

MAKES ABOUT 1 LITRE

INGREDIENTS

1kg white fish bones and trimmings (ideally turbot, halibut, sole or haddock)

2 tablespoons olive oil

1 small onion, peeled and chopped roughly

½ celery stalk, trimmed and sliced

1 small fennel bulb, trimmed and sliced

1 small leek, trimmed and sliced

Sea salt and black pepper to season

100ml dry white wine

METHOD

If using fish heads, make sure to remove the eyes and gills, and remove any traces of blood.

Heat the olive oil in a stock pot or large saucepan and add the onion, celery, fennel, leek and a little salt and pepper. Stir over a medium heat for 3–4 minutes until the vegetables begin to soften, but don't let them brown. Add the fish bones and wine and let the liquid bubble until it has reduced by half.

Pour in enough cold water to cover everything and bring to the boil, then skim off the scum from the surface.

Lower the heat and simmer for 20 minutes. Remove the pan from the heat and allow the stock to settle for about 20 minutes as it cools.

Ladle the stock through a muslin-lined sieve into a large bowl. Chill and use within 2–3 days, or freeze in small quantities for up to 3 months.

Beef Stock

MAKES ABOUT 1 LITRE

INGREDIENTS

1.75kg beef bones with marrow

4 carrots, chopped

4 celery stalks, chopped

2 medium onions, unpeeled and quartered

4 cloves of garlic, unpeeled and smashed

1 teaspoon sea salt

1 teaspoon whole peppercorns

2 bay leaves

3 sprigs of fresh thyme

5–6 sprigs of parsley

1 tablespoon tomato purée

METHOD

Preheat the oven to 200°C/425°F/gas mark 7, then roast your beef bones for 25–30 minutes.

Once the bones are ready, place all the ingredients in a really large saucepan. Pour in enough cold water to cover and bring to a boil over a high heat, then reduce the heat and simmer gently, occasionally skimming the fat that rises to the surface. Simmer on a very low heat for 24–48 hours to extract all the goodness from the bones. I know it sounds like a long time but, trust me, it's worth it. If you are time poor,

6 hours will do on a medium heat to simmer.

Remove from the heat and allow to cool slightly. Strain the liquid through a colander into a bowl, discarding the solids. Let the broth cool slightly.

Ladle the broth through a muslin-lined sieve into a large bowl. Chill and use within 2–3 days, or freeze in small quantities for up to 3 months.

Vegetable Stock

MAKES ABOUT 1.5 LITRES

INGREDIENTS

3 onions, peeled and roughly chopped

1 leek, washed, peeled and chopped

2 celery sticks, chopped

6 carrots, peeled and chopped

½ bulb of garlic, cut in half, skin on

½ teaspoon black peppercorns

A good handful of mixed herbs (e.g. thyme, tarragon and parsley)

1 bay leaf

200ml dry white wine

Sea salt to season

METHOD

Put all the vegetables into a large stock pot along with the garlic and peppercorns. Pour in enough cold water to cover, around 2 litres, and bring to the boil.

Lower the heat to simmer gently for 20 minutes. Remove the pan from the heat and then add the herbs, bay leaf and the wine and season lightly with sea salt.

Give it a really good stir and allow to cool completely. If you have time, chill the stock overnight before straining. Otherwise pass it through a fine sieve once cooled. Use within 5 days, or freeze in batches for up to 3 months.

Chicken Stock

MAKES ABOUT 1.5 LITRES

INGREDIENTS

2 tablespoons olive oil
1 carrot, peeled and chopped
1 onion, peeled and chopped
2 celery sticks, chopped
1 small leek, peeled, washed and chopped
3 cloves of garlic, skin on, cut in half
2 bay leaves
4–5 sprigs of thyme
2 tablespoons tomato purée
2 tablespoons plain flour
1kg raw chicken bones (roast them for 30 minutes if making a brown chicken stock)
Sea salt to season

METHOD

Heat the olive oil in a large stock pot over a high heat and fry off the vegetables, garlic, bay leaves and thyme. Stir occasionally until they colour.

Stir in the tomato purée and flour and cook for a minute, then add the chicken bones and pour in enough cold water to cover them. Season really lightly.

Bring to the boil and skim off any scum and froth that rises to the surface with a large spoon. Reduce the heat to a simmer and leave to cook really gently for about an hour. Let it settle and cool for 30 minutes before passing it through a fine sieve. Chill and use within 4–5 days, or freeze in batches for up to 3 months.

Olive Tapenade

MAKES 300G

INGREDIENTS

40g can of anchovy fillets, drained
200g pitted black olives
2 tablespoons capers
1 large clove of garlic, peeled and crushed
1 tablespoon olive oil, plus extra for storing

METHOD

Whiz all the ingredients in a food processor until smooth. Store in a jar topped with a drizzle of olive oil. Chill and use within a week.

Oven-Dried Tomatoes

MAKES 300G

INGREDIENTS
300g cherry vine tomatoes, halved
Sea salt
4–5 sprigs of fresh thyme
Olive oil

METHOD
Preheat the oven to 90°C/225°F/gas mark ¼.

Lay the tomatoes with the seeds up on a tray lined with some parchment paper. Season with sea salt and then scatter with the thyme leaves. Drizzle with olive oil and bake in the oven for 4 hours.

Allow to cool, then refrigerate. Use within a week.

Red Wine Jus

This is a super master recipe that can be adapted for any meat dish. It works great with lamb and beef. If you are having chicken, try using Madeira wine instead, or if cooking duck add some spices such as cinnamon and star anise. You can make this in advance and reheat just before it is needed.

MAKES 600ML

INGREDIENTS
300ml red wine
2 sprigs of fresh thyme
2 sprigs of fresh rosemary
100ml balsamic vinegar (sometimes I add cherry balsamic for a different flavour)
2 tablespoons honey
600ml beef stock
1 tablespoon cornflour, mixed with 3 tablespoons water (optional)

METHOD
In a good-sized saucepan, add the red wine and herbs. Boil on a high heat until reduced by half, then add the balsamic vinegar and honey, and reduce slightly again. This normally takes about 5 minutes.

Add the beef stock, bring to the boil and thicken by reduction or with the cornflour. Taste and make sure it has the right balance of sweet and sour. Sometimes, you may need to adjust by adding a little more vinegar or honey.

Pass through a sieve right before serving.

Balsamic/ Poached Pear/ Mango Gel

MAKES 300ML

INGREDIENTS
300ml of the required liquid (balsamic vinegar/ poached pear liquid/shop-bought mango coulis)
Ultratex

METHOD
Place the required liquid into a mixing bowl. There is no real set recipe for this as ultratex will react differently with every liquid. So the best way of making these gels is by adding a tablespoon of it at a time, whisking it into the liquid until you get the consistency of a gel that holds.

Place it into a squeezy bottle and pipe onto plates as needed. The gel can be stored in the fridge for 4–5 days.

Spun Sugar

MAKES 6–8

INGREDIENTS
200g caster sugar
1 teaspoon powdered glucose
200ml water

METHOD
Place the sugar, glucose and water into a small, heavy-based saucepan. Bring to the boil and then reduce the heat and simmer for 10–15 minutes until the mixture turns a golden caramel colour. Please don't stir the sugar as you will disrupt the caramel.

Once it reaches 160°C on your sugar thermometer, place the saucepan bottom in a bowl of cold water to cool the caramel quickly. It will thicken a little as it cools, but if it gets too thick, simply heat again and it will quickly loosen. The sugar syrup should have a thick honey consistency but it should also not be too runny.

Dip a small metal spoon into the caramel. The sugar syrup should slowly drop off the spoon. Spiral the caramel around the body of a knife-sharpening steel. Once cooled and hardened, remove the spiral from the steel carefully. Now use as a wow factor to decorate any dessert.

Passion Fruit Sorbet

Unfortunately, you can't make this without an ice-cream churner, but it's well worth investing in one if you love sorbets, as this is as good or better than anything you'll buy from a shop. I normally churn my sorbets before any guests arrive to save time.

SERVES 6

INGREDIENTS
200g caster sugar
200ml water
1½ tablespoons liquid glucose
500ml shop-bought passion fruit coulis

METHOD
Put the sugar and water into a heavy-based saucepan. Add the liquid glucose and heat gently until the sugar dissolves. Increase the heat and boil the syrup for 5 minutes until slightly thickened.

Cool completely and then mix in the passion fruit coulis. Pour the mixture into an ice-cream machine and churn until almost firm.

Transfer to a suitable container and freeze until firm. About 30 minutes before serving, transfer the sorbet to the fridge so it can be scooped easily.

Raspberry Sorbet

Although this sorbet can be made without an ice-cream maker, I find that it is best when made with one.

SERVES 4–6

INGREDIENTS
500g fresh raspberries
200ml cold water
125g caster sugar

METHOD
Put the raspberries into a blender or food processor with half of the water and mix until smooth on a medium speed. Strain through a sieve into a large bowl.

Put the remaining water into a small saucepan with the sugar and heat, stirring until the sugar dissolves. Allow the syrup to cool.

Stir the syrup into the raspberry purée then pour into a container. There are two methods of freezing the sorbet. For the best results I recommend using an ice-cream maker to churn. Allow it to churn until you have the consistency of scoopable sorbet and transfer to a container and into the freezer until you are ready to serve.

If you don't have an ice-cream maker, cover the purée and freeze for 45 minutes, then scoop the mixture into a blender jug and give it a few pulses to break it up. Repeat this process twice, then leave to freeze solid.

About 30 minutes before serving, transfer the sorbet to the fridge so it can be scooped easily.

Vanilla Ice Cream

As with the passion fruit sorbet, you can't make this without an ice-cream churner, but for this ice cream it's definitely worth the investment.

SERVES 6–8

INGREDIENTS
1 large vanilla pod
300ml full-fat milk
300ml cream
100g caster sugar
4 egg yolks

METHOD
Place a large plastic container in the freezer before you start.

Split the vanilla pod lengthways, scrape the seeds out with the point of the knife and tip into a small saucepan with the milk, cream and pod.

Bring to the boil, then remove from the heat and leave to infuse for at least 20 minutes. For the best flavour this can be done a few hours beforehand and left to go cold.

In a large bowl, whisk the sugar and egg yolks together for a few minutes until they turn pale and fluffy. Put the vanilla cream back on the heat until it is just about to boil, then carefully pour the liquid onto the yolks, beating with the whisk until completely mixed. Strain this liquid with a sieve to remove any lumps and pour it back into the saucepan.

Cook on the lowest heat your hob can go, stirring slowly and continuously with a wooden spoon, making sure the spoon touches the bottom of the pan, for about 5–10 minutes until thickened. A tip is to check using the back of the wooden spoon – if the custard is thick enough to coat it, then it is ready.

Pour the custard into a bowl and leave to cool. To stop the mix from forming a skin, make sure you put a layer of cling film directly on top of the custard.

Once cool, remove the cling film and put the custard into an ice-cream machine. Allow it to churn until a creamy, scoopable ice cream is formed. Transfer to the plastic container and freeze until you are serving.

Chocolate and Hazelnut Ice Cream

An ice cream that everyone is guaranteed to like. The Nutella just makes it.

SERVES 6–8

INGREDIENTS
550ml milk
35g liquid glucose
8 large egg yolks
25g caster sugar
200g Nutella

METHOD
Place a large plastic container in the freezer before you start.

Put the milk and liquid glucose into a saucepan and stir over a low heat until the glucose has melted. Slowly bring to the boil.

Beat the egg yolks and sugar together in a bowl, and then stir in the Nutella with a spatula. The Nutella will be quite thick.

As soon as the milk starts to boil take it straight off the heat and slowly pour into the egg mixture, whisking until smooth. Pass through a fine sieve and pour back into the saucepan.

Stir over a low heat until the custard thickens enough to coat the back of a wooden spoon. Place into a bowl and allow to cool with a layer of cling film on top of the custard to stop a skin from forming.

Once cool, remove the cling film and put the custard into an ice-cream machine. Allow it to churn until almost firm, transfer to the plastic container and freeze until you are serving.

INDEX